# UNION POWER

## AND THE PUBLIC INTEREST

**"We are all made poorer by the power of the labor unions,"** says noted economist Emerson Schmidt. Here is the first book to offer an in-depth examination of the market power of the labor union and its effect on our economy and you, the consumer.

The monopoly power of the labor union is causing inflation and other economic dislocations, which in turn require more governmental control over human action, says the author. Labor laws have effectively exempted labor organizations and their officers and members from the discipline of market competition. He tells how the wage-push, strikes, and violence force labor remuneration above rises in productivity; this leads to higher prices. It causes unemployment. Ultimately the non-striking worker as well as you, the consumer, are hurt by all this, confronted with inconveniences, rising prices, and accentuated international balance-of-payment problems.

What legal limits should be placed on union demands? What about strikes; is there a moral right to them? Should the power of the union official and the labor union be dispersed? How can the free competitive market work more effectively to the benefit of the consumer? Dr. Schmidt explores these and countless other questions which are of public interest, and he sets forth a series of corrective measures

# UNION POWER

# AND THE PUBLIC INTEREST

## BY DR. EMERSON P. SCHMIDT

NASH PUBLISHING,
LOS ANGELES

The author is indebted to Mr. Kenneth S. Templeton, Jr., Secretary of the Principles of Freedom Committee, for advice and encouragement; to Dr. John V. Van Sickle goes great thanks for many hours of work which have materially improved the writing and the substantive quality of this work; but the author, alone, is responsible for any error and weakness, as well as for the conclusions and recommendations.

Library of Congress Catalog Card Number: 72-95239
Standard Book Number: 8402-5004-5

Published simultaneously in the United States and Canada by Nash Publishing Corporation, 9255 Sunset Boulevard, Los Angeles, California 90069.

Printed in the United States of America.

First Printing.

*This volume is a publication of*
*The Principles of Freedom Committee*

The great body of economic and political literature since World War II—both academic and popular—has presented a misleading picture of the performance of private enterprise and of the State in the economies of the free world. This literature exaggerates the defects of the one and the merits of the other. Freedom will remain in jeopardy unless the public gains a clearer picture of the workings of the free market and comes to realize that its greatest virtue is not its extraordinary capacity to produce widely diffused material benefits, important as this merit is, but its unique capacity to protect the great immaterial values of our Western Heritage.

As a means of increasing the flow of literature that would correct the picture and strengthen the foundations of freedom, a group calling itself the Principles of Freedom Committee was formed during the early 1960s to promote a series of books dealing with important economic and political issues of the day. To assist in the international publication and distribution of the books, the Committee recruited an advisory group of scholars from sixteen countries. *Union Power and the Public Interest* is the seventh book in the Principles of Freedom Series.

The membership of the Committee has changed over the years through retirements and replacements by cooption. The original members were Professors Milton Friedman, F. A. Hayek, G. Warren Nutter, B. A. Rogge, and John V. Van Sickle, Executive Secretary; Ruth Sheldon Knowles, Project Coordinator; and

Byron K. Trippet, Committee Member Ex-Officio. Dr. Trippet retired in 1965 following his resignation as President of Wabash College. Professors Hayek and Nutter retired in 1968, and three new members were added: Gottfried Haberler, Galen L. Stone Professor of International Trade, Harvard University; F. A. Harper, President, Institute for Humane Studies; and Don Paarlberg, Hillenbrand Professor of Agricultural Economics, Purdue University. In 1970 Gottfried Dietze, Professor of Political Science at The Johns Hopkins University, joined the Committee, and Kenneth S. Templeton, Jr., assumed the duties of Executive Secretary from Dr. Van Sickle.

The original Committee requested modest nonrecurring grants from a number of corporations and foundations. These donors receive copies of all books as they appear, and their help in promoting the distribution of the books is welcomed. The Institute for Humane Studies handles the funds received from the project's supporters and issues annual reports. Decisions as to authors, subjects, and acceptability of manuscripts rest exclusively with the Committee.

Earlier volumes in the Principles of Freedom Series are:

*Great Myths of Economics* (1968) by Don Paarlberg

*The Strange World of Ivan Ivanov* (1969) by G. Warren Nutter

*Freedom in Jeopardy: The Tyranny of Idealism* (1969) by John V. Van Sickle

*The Regulated Consumer* (1971) by Mary Bennett Peterson

*The Genius of the West* (1971) by Louis Rougier

# CONTENTS

# UNION POWER
# AND THE PUBLIC INTEREST

# WHAT IS
# THE LABOR UNION
# PROBLEM?

In 1776, Adam Smith said:

> People of the same trade seldom meet together, even for
> merriment and diversion, but the conversation ends in a
> conspiracy against the public or in some contrivance to
> raise prices.

In 1944, Professor Henry C. Simons of the University of Chicago
said:

> No one and no group can be trusted with much power; and
> it is merely silly to complain because groups exercise
> power selfishly. . . . Monopoly power must be abused. It
> has no use save abuse.

Adam Smith was thinking of business and businessmen. Henry
Simons was thinking of trade unions and collective bargaining. But
his strictures apply with equal force to business.

Were Adam Smith living today, he would undoubtedly include
trade unions in his indictment. "Workers of the same trade," he
might say now, "seldom meet together, even for a picnic or a beer,
but the conversation ends in a conspiracy against the consumer, or in
some contrivance to raise wages and reduce output."

The issues that concerned Adam Smith were forcefully, though
not perfectly, met by the enactment of the Sherman Antitrust Act of
July 2, 1890. This law provided that:

3

> Every contract, combination in the form of trust or other-
> wise, or conspiracy, in restraint of trade or commerce
> among the several states, or with foreign nations, is hereby
> declared to be illegal.

"Every contract" was the phrase used. That the Congress had more than business in mind is suggested by other clauses of the act. "Every person who makes such a contract is guilty . . ." and again, "Every person who shall monopolize, or attempt to monopolize or combine, or conspire with any other person or persons . . . shall be deemed guilty. . . ."

More than half of the state constitutions have antimonopoly provisions; nearly all states have their own antitrust laws.

For over forty years antitrust laws applied to the activities of unions quite as much as to those of private businesses—perhaps more so, because of the frequency with which union activities threatened irreparable damage to property rights, which the courts held to be as deserving of respect as human rights. This impartiality continued, despite the declaration in the 1914 amendment to the Sherman Antitrust Act (the Clayton Act) that labor was not a commodity or article of commerce, and that labor organizations should not be held or construed to be illegal combinations or conspiracies in restraint of trade under the antitrust laws.

This declaration appears to have been based on the assumption that competition in product markets protected consumers and hence workers as consumers, but did not protect them as workers. With the coming of the Great Depression and the New Deal in the 1930s, when unionized labor was the cornerstone of a coalition of special-interest groups, that assumption came close to being accepted as a self-evident truth. The labor laws of the 1930s, described in later chapters, are the products of this assumption. As we shall see, they effectively exempted labor organizations, their officers and their members from the discipline of market competition.[1]

---

1. For a brief account of labor and antitrust laws, see *Origin of Antitrust Immunity for Labor Unions* (Washington: Chamber of Commerce of U.S.A., 1962).

Check·

4

## MAJOR COMPLAINTS AGAINST LABOR UNIONS

But before we examine the wisdom of the extension of the legal immunities and exemptions to labor unions beginning in the 1930s, let us take a quick look at the chief complaints now made against unions and union officials.

Opinion Research Corporation, widely recognized for its objectivity in measuring public opinion, reported in May 1972 that over half the public believed labor unions have grown too powerful, and more than two-thirds that strikes and labor troubles have seriously hurt the country.[2]

Labor unions come in many sizes, with greatly variegated styles, leadership, outlook, power, and impact, so that any generalizations about them may be subject to challenge. There will inevitably be exceptions and qualifications to every broad conclusion. In what follows, that fact should be kept in mind.

Most appraisals of unions are made from limited impressions and experiences or casual observation. They may be biased, shallow, and inaccurate. A systematic, objective study is needed.

The late Professor Joseph A. Schumpeter of Harvard pointed out that a comprehensive analysis of an economic condition in a society consists of two complementary but distinct elements: (1) the theorist's view of the basic features of the conditions of the society, and what is important and what is not, in order to understand its nature at a given time; and (2) the analyst's technic or mental apparatus which suggests concrete propositions or "theories." From the latter, then, he may make clear what changes might well be sought.[3]

Applying this approach to society's labor-union problems, what basic features are now evident? So-called free collective bargaining has become compulsory collective bargaining. Voluntary union membership has been largely superseded by the union shop. Unions have accumulated a vast array of legal immunities and exemptions (from

---

2. See AP story, for example, *Washington Evening Star,* 30 May 1972.

3. Joseph A. Schumpeter, *Ten Great Economists* (New York: Oxford University Press, 1951).

5

antitrust laws and injunctions, for example) that set them above their employers and the consumer.

The work ethic has been denigrated. The union official evaluates his worth to union members by gains not in production and output but in what he can wangle for them *to use off the job:* more money, higher pensions and earlier retirement, broader insurance coverage, and more paid holidays and vacations. The joy, creativity, and sense of participation in work are downgraded. Productivity, quality, reliability, and accountability get low ratings.

Featherbedding—particularly in printing and publishing, transportation, and construction—is not only condoned, but defended. Output limitations are a matter of course. In skilled trades and some professions, apprenticeship quotas and other restrictions on entry are rife.

The accumulation of strike funds and a readiness to call strikes and prolong them are taken for granted, with the threat or actual use of coercion and violence always looming. Retailers, dealers, employers, and consumers are assumed not to have any right to continuity of service and output. The union official, furthermore, seeks and gets government subsidies for strikers: food stamps, welfare payments, and unemployment compensation; aid from charitable organizations may also be available.

He seeks a higher legal minimum wage for all to help push up the entire wage structure. He favors higher import duties and import quotas. The combined effect of these policies is to drive up costs of production, to induce a serious misuse and misallocation of resources, and to generate unemployment. They also contribute to domestic divisiveness and hostility, reduce output, and aggravate the imbalance in our international payments accounts.

Labor costs, directly and indirectly, account for 75 percent of the cost of all products but the union official tends to see labor costs only as members' income. Employers (consumers) see them both as income to workers and as costs that must be covered in the sales price and in other outlays of the final consumer.

Labor unions have created special problems in the government sector. Here the union officials sit, in effect, *on both sides of the*

6

*bargaining table.* In many cases they elect, or play a dominant role in electing, top officials in the executive branch—federal, state, and local—as well as in the legislative branch, who then support them in their demands on the public purse. This is not collective bargaining as that is usually conceived; it is effective union control of the employer—in this case, the public officials who directly or indirectly enter into contracts with the unions.

Because of the extreme diversity in union leadership and union power and the diverse economic, political, and social environment of various unions, the results of sectional bargaining cannot be expected to yield equity or justice in wages[4] and other working conditions among the different unions. Both the president and the secretary-treasurer of the AFL-CIO have repeatedly asserted that they were not concerned about the limited percentage of all workers who belong to unions.

Yet, today, unions are widely spread across most industries and are found not only in cities, but also in small towns, counties, and villages. A relatively minor movement before World War II, unionism has since gone nearly everywhere, and will expand, particularly in the fast-growing public sector. This means that those who view unions with some alarm will have increasing cause for concern. Settlements of union demands tend to raise the expectations of the rest of the labor force.

Labor-union literature—newspapers, magazines, pamphlets, leaflets, tapes, and movies—poured out by the millions of copies day after day, is seriously misleading as to economic facts and relationships. The General Electric Corporation has made maximum efforts to offset that outpouring. Neither employers, generally, nor the public schools have done anything to set the record straight.

The foregoing provides a brief preview of the issues and topics to be analyzed in the remainder of this study. A book by Haynes Johnson and Nick Kotz, *Washington Post* writers, based on taped

---

4. Throughout this study the term *wages* is generally used to include so-called fringes or wage supplements.

interviews with union officials, members, nonmembers, employers, and others, emphasizes many if not most of the same points.[5]

In a single sentence: the public problem is to cut down the accumulated power of labor unions. Put another way: the problem is the restoration of competition in the labor market.

This raises the question as to whether we were right in the 1930s to extend antitrust exemptions to unions and to build up a complex of other government supports for unionization. The answer to this question depends on answers to several others. What is competition? How effective is it in the goods market? Is it true that, while antitrust laws, vigorously enforced, can prevent businesses from gaining monopoly power, the same laws applied with equal vigor to labor unions would destroy them or damage the working man by precluding him from getting a fair share of the returns from production, on a par with landowners, suppliers of capital, and management?

## THE ROLE OF COMPETITION

Does the free competitive market readily pass the gains from new discoveries and technology on to employees and consumers in the form of higher income or lower prices, or both? Or do other income claimants get them? The answers to such questions will largely determine whether we have now reached a point in history when we should rely on more competition in the labor market.

---

5. After this work was virtually complete, *The Washington Post* published a series of ten articles by Haynes Johnson and Nick Kotz, the paper's staff writers, beginning April 9, 1972, and concluding April 18th, on unions, employers, and the public interest. These articles seem to be quite objective. Congressman S. P. Lloyd had them inserted in the *Congressional Record,* May 3, 1972, pages E 4642-61, available from the Government Printing Office for twenty-five cents. The criticisms and evaluations in this series parallel closely those of this volume, although the authors do not advance many corrective policies. Their work merits careful consideration, particularly by anyone who has reservations in regard to the analysis here. See, *The Unions,* Haynes Johnson and Nick Kotz (New York: Pocket Books) recently released.

The key to effective competition in business is freedom of entry by new producers and new suppliers of identical or similar products and services. So long as existing producers and suppliers are everlastingly in danger of being replaced by newcomers from within the country or from abroad, prices, largely reflecting costs, will tend to be competitive.

Competition is generally not perfect nor "pure" in the sense that producers are so small a part of the total market in an industry that the output of any one of them has no perceptible effect on price, as in the case of a wheat farmer, for example. Actually, such a "model" of perfect competition is used by economics-textbook writers and teachers as a starting point, merely to contrast it with varying degrees of market power or with monopoly.

Some use the phrase *monopolistic-competition* to characterize our economy. The late Professor John M. Clark of Columbia concluded that our goal should be "workable competition." Preventing monopoly by law, encouraging science and new technology, and removing the barriers to new entry would pave the way for effective competition.

The monopolist, just like competitive producers taken together, faces downward, negative-sloping demand curves. This is a fancy way of saying that at higher prices, he will sell less; at lower prices, he will sell more. Under vigorous competition, selling prices tend to coincide with costs; under monopoly, output is controlled so that profits are maximized. The consumer benefits most when competition is widespread and vigorous; output is larger and prices are lower than under monopoly.

But even monopolists generally face substitutes, or the consumer may do without if he regards the price as too high. Markets tend to be neither perfectly competitive nor completely monopolized. Occasionally outright collusion occurs. More often, trade names, copyrights, patents, or product differentiation (as among soaps, lotions, appliances, or apparel) may insulate the producer from the full rigors of competition. Tariffs and import quotas reduce foreign competition.

Our type of economy, with private ownership of the instruments of production, is justified primarily because of the heavy reliance on competition in the goods market and the widespread freedom of entry by new enterprises.

We rely on competition to stimulate business efficiency, to encourage innovations and variety, and to cater to a wide range of tastes and desires among consumers. We have some ten million separate enterprises, most of which are small sole proprietorships. Some are cooperatives, and more are partnerships. Less than 10 percent are corporations, although corporations do more than 75 percent of all business. Any enterprise can prosper only by catering to free-choice consumers. Advertising and sales promotion influence, but cannot dominate, buyers. The sizable mortality rate among products and producers demonstrates this. Studying the rise and fall of products and companies, a Brookings Institution report stated, "The top is a slippery place."

The records of the antitrust division of the office of the attorney general, of the Federal Trade Commission, and of some other government agencies, abound with cases involving attempts to reduce competition, or of price-fixing by business rivals. Mergers and acquisitions have been questioned or disallowed because they reduced, or might substantially reduce, competition.

Some states allow manufacturers to set retail prices. Congress has passed a law requiring automobile manufacturers or their dealers to attach the "suggested list price" on each vehicle offered for sale. Customs tariffs and import quotas reduce foreign competition; but such limitations may actually step up domestic investment and enhance competition. Government regulations place floors under prices of certain agricultural products, and under rates charged by carriers.

Patents and copyrights create temporary monopolies, but by stimulating creative effort and new investment, they usually have an opposite impact over time. Trade names, trademarks, and product variations may have similar long-run results. Building codes, formerly rather restrictive, now tend to stress performance standards rather than specific materials or products. They now encourage modular construction, precutting, preassembly, and prefabrication—unless construction trades block such cost-cutting innovations.

10

## WIDENING CONSUMER CHOICES

Our economy has elements of both monopoly and competition, but it is probably more competitive than monopolistic. Certainly the range of choices, both among manufacturers as buyers and among final consumers, has widened enormously in the twentieth century.

Transportation by horse-drawn vehicles, railroad trains, and boats, has been replaced or supplemented by pipelines, automobiles, buses and trucks, and airlines. Both people and goods are much more mobile. Compared to forty or fifty years ago, the real cost of transportation has sharply declined, thus enhancing competition. Our tariffs on imports have been cut to the point where the United States is a low-tariff country. In 1970, of our $40 billion worth of imports, some $14 billion were duty-free. The average tariff on dutiable products dropped from nearly 47 percent in 1934 to 9 percent in 1971. The duty on all imported goods, dutiable and free, dropped from 18.4 percent to under 6.5 percent in the same period.

The flood of Japanese, other Oriental, and European imports— automobiles, radios, television sets, typewriters, bicycles, motor-cycles, sewing machines, umbrellas, textiles, etc.—attests to the transformation in recent decades.

New discoveries in the chemical industry have left few other industries or products unchanged in the past generation. Wool and cotton, for example, are rivaled by a host of synthetic fibers for apparel, carpeting, upholstering and seat covers, drapes and curtains. In construction, iron and steel compete with several other metals, particularly copper and aluminum; with wood, particle board, laminated woods, and plywood; with glass, ceramics, concrete (including prestressed concrete); with synthetic boards, asphalt products, and numerous plastics. Synthetic diamonds are available for industrial cutting purposes. A modern supermarket carries eight- to ten-thousand different items, offering a range of choices that is the envy of the world. Discount stores dominate some retail fields and operate in virtually all others. Special "sales" events cut many average prices below those reported by the Bureau of Labor Statistics and listed in the Consumer Price Index.

Schumpeter coined the phrase *creative destruction* to characterize the constant discovery, development, and marketing of new and different products that replace existing ones, in whole or in part. He did not argue that prevalent theories of "imperfect competition" were completely in error in regard to the economy at a particular time, but they did give a seriously misleading picture of our economy *in motion.*[6]

Schumpeter's conclusion was that when capitalism is viewed as an economy in motion, its alleged imperfections are seen as what keeps it dynamic and progressive. The successful businessman is a great agent of progress. He is the innovator. He has a goodly combination of daring, courage, self-confidence, and imagination, which enables him to raise capital and to develop and market new products and services. Profits are the rewards to those who develop and promote change. The constant procession of further innovations and changes steadily threatens the profits and survival of erstwhile innovators and leaders who are, in turn, left behind. Without temporary elements of "preferred competition" or trade names, or differentiated products, great sums of money would not and could not be risked.[7]

Thoroughgoing monopoly and monopoly profits can persist only if government provides checks on competition. Anticompetitive methods in business tend to be whittled away by rivals, unless government prevents it. Even international cartels designed by governments and producers to fix or control (*stabilize,* is the customary word) prices of key raw materials—such as rubber, coffee, tin, wheat—rarely endure long.

Economists have tried, with little success, to measure the extent of monopoly or competition by analyzing "sticky" versus "flexible" prices; the former suggesting some monopoly power and the latter active competition. Nearly all prices are administered prices—of

---

6. For an excellent evaluation of the degree of competitiveness of our economy and a discussion of Schumpeter's contribution, see John V. Van Sickle and Benjamin A. Rogge, *Introduction to Economics* (New York: D. Van Nostrand Company, 1954), p. 221.

7. Joseph A. Schumpeter, *Capitalism, Socialism, and Democracy* (New York: Harper & Bros., 1942). This book, incidentally, first published in the 1930s, predicted with great insight the disaffection of so-called intellectuals with our form of government and capitalism.

12

necessity. Others have studied levels of economic concentration as measured by the proportion of sales that a few of the largest companies in an industry account for—four companies in the automobile industry, for example. This, it is sometimes argued, makes collusion easy, or diminishes competition. Such concentration studies generally omit imports, and may therefore be seriously misleading. They also ignore in-house production—as of castings, let us say, when a giant machine shop or an automobile company also makes its own castings—or as in the case of the Ford Motor Company, which makes some of its own steel. Ford is not counted as part of the steel industry.

Professor George Stigler of the University of Chicago has been critical of his colleagues and certain lawyers who conclude from concentration studies that monopoly is widespread and is increasing, and that so-called administered prices are a source of continuous inflation, a matter discussed below.[8]

Professor M. A. Adelman of MIT, a close student of these matters, concluded as recently as 1970 that, in spite of the massive growth in size of individual companies and of the substantial waves of mergers and acquisitions, there is little or no evidence of greater concentration in our economy in the last couple of generations.[9]

Professor Peter Drucker of New York University, in an extensive analysis of recent economic and structural developments in American business, concluded that, in spite of the growth of large corporations and the development of multinational enterprises and conglomerates, our economy has become more competitive.[10]

Even though the 100 largest companies control a larger proportion of total assets in manufacturing than ten or twenty years ago, this development has increased, not decreased, competition.

Drucker stated:

---

8. See particularly Stigler's article reprinted in *Basic Economics: A Book of Readings*. Edited by A. D. Gayer, et al. (New York: Prentice-Hall, Inc., 1951), pp. 204-11. See ibid., "What Is an Industry?" Stigler's more recent findings are in *Journal of Business* (Chicago: University of Chicago Press, January 1962).

9. M. A. Adelman, "Two Faces of Economic Concentration," *The Public Interest* (New York: National Affairs, Inc., Fall 1970), pp. 117-26.

10. Peter Drucker, "The New Markets and the New Capitalism," *The Public Interest* (New York: National Affairs, Inc., Fall 1970), pp. 44-79.

The odd thing, however, is that this tremendous concentration has not been accompanied by any increase in concentration in economic power in any single market for goods, that is, in any single market in which manufacturing companies operate. In market after market, new companies have challenged the big old companies and have taken away from them a piece here or a piece there of their traditional business. This is true whether we speak of book publishing or of pharmaceuticals, of building materials or of retail sales.

If the Bureau of the Census data on the concentration of manufacturing assets were corrected for the assets that are owned by the largest companies but are not a part of their manufacturing complex, Drucker tells us, they would probably show that the companies own a smaller proportion of the actual manufacturing assets now than they did twenty years ago. That would imply increased competition. Drucker concludes that it is not without relevance that the most common criticism of multinational companies—whether they are American companies in Europe, or European and Japanese in the United States—has been that their size enables them to engage in excessive competition, not that they are monopolizing the market.

Gottfried Haberler, a Harvard professor emeritus who has written one of the most thorough analyses of income policies and inflation, concluded that in our economy, with our strong antitrust laws effectively enforced, there is no need for price controls, although the power of the labor union must be reduced.[11] Haberler believes that even if monopoly were substituted for competition in business, it would have essentially a one-shot price-lifting effect, whereas unions demand annual wage increases. He also said, "The plain fact is that the American economy is much more competitive than most people, including many economists, realize. . . ."

Haberler's conclusions accord closely with those of a group of distinguished economists appointed in the late 1950s to examine the causes of persistent inflation. They unanimously agreed that in the United States the wage push played a major role. "With demand

11. Gottfried Haberler, *Incomes Policies and Inflation* (Washington: American Enterprise Institute, 1971).

pressures less intense in the U.S.A. than in Europe, round after round of wage increases have weakened the competitive position of American industry."[12]

They also unanimously agreed that there is no counterpart on the business side to the continuous wage push—in spite of what J. K. Galbraith has been asserting for years. The Paris group said, "We believe that the danger of aggressive pricing to raise profit margins is a limited one. It can add fuel to the fire in an inflationary situation. But it is not likely to be the starting cause, nor can it be a cause of continuously rising prices. In this respect, an increase in profit margins differs from an increase in wages; there can be a wage-price spiral, but there cannot be a profit-price spiral." The economists rejected the idea that large corporations in industries having only a few companies, continuously push prices up. Competition, though not perfect, is quite effective.

The forty-year-old theory that prices on a wide front are administered by large corporations is now being severely challenged by some recent innovative research, particularly that done by Professor J. Fred Weston and associates at UCLA. Profits, they found, are not significantly higher in concentrated industries than in others. The data, analysis, and conclusions of Gardiner Means, J. K. Galbraith, and others of their school, are found dubious or incorrect.[13]

## WAGE CHANGES VERSUS PRICE CHANGES

The substantially slower rise of wholesale prices and consumer prices, relative to the rise of wage rates, suggests that the productivity gains over the years have been quite effectively passed on to buyers and consumers generally. On the average, labor compensation accounts for about 75 percent of the cost of goods sold at wholesale and retail. From 1947 to mid-1971, average hourly earnings in the private nonfarm sector of our economy increased by 204

---

12. William Fellner, et al., *The Problem of Rising Prices* (Paris: Organization for European Economic Cooperation, 1960).

13. Gilbert Burck, "The Myths and Realities of Corporate Pricing" (*Fortune* Magazine, April 1972).

percent, wholesale prices by 50 percent, and the Consumer Price Index (CPI) by 82 percent. This same relationship has prevailed for more than 150 years. It suggests that competition in the goods markets has been substantial; had monopoly predominated, monopolists would have garnered the benefits of the rise in productivity over the years.[14]  (A later chapter treats this issue more fully.)

Tentatively, we must raise the question whether the vast build-up of labor-union power came about through a major misreading of the nature of a properly functioning free-market economy. If employees almost automatically and inevitably garner the bulk of the gains of new discoveries and new technology that result in greater output per man-hour, what essential and equitable *economic* functions can a labor union perform?

The burden of proof would seem to rest on those who hold, as spokesmen of unionized labor, that the general interest is best served by exempting unions, their leaders and members, from the discipline of competition.

We have examined the workings of the competitive market under our business system because, if we expect public support for major changes in our labor laws, we must be reasonably certain that competition is effective in the goods market.

In what follows, the nature of the impasse to which we have come, and the malaise that plagues our society—and the entire Western world—are analyzed. Innumerable corrective steps are indicated, followed in the last two chapters by a summary of key suggestions.

## A WARNING NOTE

An early warning note must be posted: Corrective steps in the labor market will be undertaken only after a broad base of understanding is established, particularly among thought and opinion leaders, including those in the rank and file. It is hoped that what follows will help to establish such a base.

---

14. Here, and in much that follows, statistical data are confined to the period ending in mid-1971, because the wage-price freeze and subsequent government orders and controls played a heavy part in setting prices and wages.

The first duty of each of us is to improve his own insight and understanding. Then others will seek our advice and counsel, and a movement for workable reforms will emerge. Human freedom, liberty, and economic progress will be advanced not only for the working man, but also for all of us as consumers, as citizens, and as human beings.

Montesquieu anticipating Lord Acton warned:
"Any man with power is led to abuse it.
He will push it until it meets a limit. . . .
If power is not to be abused,
it must be checked by another power."

Quoted by Louis Rougier in
*The Genius of the West*

# UNION AIM: TAKE LABOR OUT OF COMPETITION

A generation or two ago, few union officials would have openly announced that the purpose of a labor union is to destroy competition in the labor market, or to "take labor out of competition." Today, however, unionism has been so widely accepted as a force in society that its spokesmen do not hesitate to admit that this is their purpose. The editor of *Motorman and Conductor* once told me, "One of the principles of trade unionism is to destroy competition. The only way that can be done is to organize all workers." Once the purpose of unions is understood, many related issues are clarified and take on new meaning. To eliminate competition, the union official employs innumerable tactics and strategies that impinge on the rights and interests of others.

In 1949, in a brief submitted to the United States Supreme Court opposing state right-to-work laws, the A.F. of L. argued that "workers cannot thrive but can only die under competition between themselves," and must have "the right to eliminate wage competition."[1]

Arthur Goldberg, labor union counsel and secretary of the Department of Labor in the 1960s, put the matter this way:

---

1. Donald R. Richberg, "Labor Monopoly Rests on Violence," *Human Events,* Washington, Oct. 27, 1956.

Technically speaking, any labor union is a monopoly in the limited sense that it eliminates competition between workingmen for the available jobs in a particular plant or industry. After all, all unions are combinations of workingmen to increase, by concerted economic action, their wages, i.e., the price at which the employer will be able to purchase their labors.[2]

And Professor Donald Watson, in one of the standard college textbooks, *Economic Policy: Government and Business,* states, "At the outset, let it be clear that unions limit competition among their members. This is the meaning, the very essence of collective bargaining."

Addressing itself to the market (monopoly) power of the labor union, the Committee for Economic Development (CED) wrote:

Typically, the employees of several, or most or sometimes all employers in a particular industry or labor market, or all the workers in a particular craft, are joined together in one union. It has been the major objective of American unions to achieve a position in which they represent the employees of all competing employers. This is known as "taking labor out of competition." This goes beyond providing workers with a defense against "unilateral" or arbitrary action of their employers. It means preventing employers from competing with each other in the sale of products on the basis of the terms on which they employ labor.[3]

The CED makes it clear that to have monopoly powers, a union need not have hundreds of thousands, or even thousands, of members. A small number of workers controlling the supply of a type of labor essential to the production of something for which there is no

---

2. From Arthur Goldberg, *AFL-CIO: Labor United* (New York: McGraw-Hill Book Co., 1956), p. 157. Professors Armen A. Alchian and Wm. R. Allen, *University Economics* (Belmont, California: Wadsworth Publishing Co., 1964 ed.), p. 502, wonder, "Why did he write *'technically* speaking' and 'in the *limited* sense'? Is there some other mode of speaking and is there an unlimited sense of monopoly?"

3. CED, *Union Powers and Union Functions: Toward a Better Balance* (New York: CED, 1964).

close substitute can be extremely powerful, as fifteen garage mechanics, striking *The Evening Star* in Washington, D.C., on New Year's Eve 1970, demonstrated. A small group can close down vast operations, throw large numbers of workers out of their jobs, or exact enormous rewards by merely threatening to do so. As John Davenport, formerly an editor of *Fortune* magazine and a life-long student of labor economics and trade unionism, has put it, "By its very nature a union seeks to monopolize the supply of labor in a given firm or industry." Neither Davenport nor the other sources quoted above are antiunion, incidentally.

This interpretation of the labor union's function is further confirmed by the concept "*collective* bargaining." To bargain means, according to Webster's dictionary, to try to get, buy, or sell something on favorable terms, to haggle. The adjective *collective* conveys the idea that numerous buyers or sellers are uniting in the bargaining. If this were the only difference between bargaining and collective bargaining, there would be a few misgivings about the latter, and this book would never have been written, or if written, never read. Even a union demand followed by a strike (and nothing else) would raise few eyebrows.

In the view of the union official, no painter, paperhanger, or pressman should be allowed to work for less than the union rate in a given labor market. Anyone who opposes or deviates downward from the union rate meets with the epithet *scab, union-buster,* or *fink.* The aim of the union official is to create a monopoly of the craft or industrial skill or trade covered by his union.

He may argue, of course, that his purpose is merely to seek "equality of bargaining power" with the employer. But union strategy and tactics are always directed toward one end: to win; to drive the employer into a corner; to wrest from him a bigger "settlement" than ever before.

The viability of an economy depends heavily on workers' and industries' creating values—exchange values, which lead to the expansion of willing exchanges—so that all can benefit from the division of labor. Wage distortions, cost distortions, monopoly distortions reduce the exchange viability of the economy. On the domestic front, this was the major reason why in mid-August 1971, President Nixon did an about-face and instituted a ninety-day wage-price freeze. The union officials, who were largely responsible for crippling this essential viability, cried out loudest against the freeze.

## UNION POWER

To be powerful and effective, union officials need to cover the field. Dual unions—two unions aspiring to cover the same trade—fight each other vigorously. Union officials seek to establish a closed shop, under which no nonunion man can work; or a union shop under which the nonunion man may work only a few days—usually thirty or less—after which, under the law and the typical union contract, the worker can be thrown off the job if he fails to join the union. Where a right-to-work law bars compulsory unionism, the so-called agency shop may be enforced. Here the nonunion man must nevertheless pay financial tribute to the union of his unchoosing. Section 14(b) of the Taft-Hartley Act reaffirms the right of the states to pass laws against compulsory unionism.

Clearly, there may be conflicts of interests and views between employees and employer on right-to-work laws, the open and closed shop, and the agency shop. If competition among employers and employees were effective, if law and order were fully maintained by government, and there were no compulsion on the employer to bargain collectively; then there would be complete freedom among the parties to agree *voluntarily* on open-versus-closed shop, right-to-work policies, and the like. Because government has failed to remain neutral in these matters, most employers and numerous states favor retaining their options on them.[4]

In some cases, unions close their rolls to new members. High initiation fees reduce the number of craftsmen. Long apprenticeship periods help to thin out the number of available craftsmen. In the skilled crafts, the union, either through its own powers or by contract with employers, limits the ratio of apprentices to journeymen.

---

4. See Milton Friedman, *Capitalism and Freedom* (Chicago: University of Chicago Press, 1962), p. 115.

Some city ordinances specify that only "qualified" craftsmen may be employed on certain types of work, and in many communities the products of vocational or career schools do not rate as qualified.

Through occupational licensure, states and municipalities have raised barriers to entry into semiskilled, skilled, and professional occupations. By 1952, more than eighty separate occupations had been given this treatment; North Carolina extended its law to sixty occupations. Usually, regard for safety, health, and similar high-sounding motives were advanced for the policy. It is not surprising that in nearly all cases the trade or profession covered sets the standards for entry, and administers the law or ordinance—usually without the consumer being even vaguely aware of the burden imposed on him.[5]

In 1972 the Justice Department filed an antitrust suit charging the American Institute of Architects with fee fixing, and in effect, "taking architects out of competition." A "code of standards" had prohibited members from making competitive bids for their services.[6] Similar actions were taken against an association of civil engineers, and another against an association of accountants. Officials in the Justice Department have issued warnings in regard to price or fee fixing by lawyers' and doctors' associations, but somewhat comparable union actions flourish unmolested.

Union boycotts are designed to block the movement of output from nonunion establishments. Secondary boycotts aim at third parties not involved in a specific union's demand of its employer. "Hot cargo" spells out another union weapon. Even when outlawed, such union devices are often most effective in eliminating unwanted workmen or output from enterprises that are anathema to the union officials. Restricting recruitment to union hiring halls, often by stipulations written into contracts, help greatly to destroy competition in the labor market.

In a union milieu, the life of a nonunion worker is no bed of roses. Frequently, mild request or persuasion, if not heeded by the worker,

5. Ibid.
6. *Washington Evening Star*, 18 May 1972. For a bitter editorial see, *Architectural Forum*, June 1972, p. 21.

is soon followed by more forceful techniques, including persistent nagging, ridicule, embarrassment, harassment, and such coercive devices as midnight telephone calls and threats to his person and family. Union officials and organizers are schooled and drilled in these techniques. In many cases, anything goes, as was forcefully brought out in *Crime Without Punishment* by Senator John L. McClellan. The senator's findings were based on months of hearings before the Senate Select Committee on Improper Activities in the Labor and Management Field; Senator McClellan acknowledged indebtedness for the work to the chief counsel of the committee, Robert F. Kennedy. The tactics that even a so-called good union will resort to (United Automobile Workers under Walter Reuther) are documented in the hundreds of acts of violence by the United Automobile Workers union against the Kohler Company.[7]

## EQUALIZING BARGAINING POWER?

Labor-union partisans often invoke the concept of "equalizing bargaining power between employers and unions." That appeals as a noble goal—soothing, calming, even relaxing. But Professor Donald Watson has denounced the phrase because it has no precise meaning. Professor Edward S. Mason of Harvard advised that the doctrine of equality of bargaining power be quietly buried, because of the impossibility of measuring amounts of bargaining power, because of its implications of stalemate, and because the doctrine has no necessary bearing on the efficient operation of the economy.[8]

Union officialdom is not actually concerned with equality of bargaining power; it is concerned with keeping enough strength, potential threat, and power to enforce its demands. Demands may

---

7. Sylvester Petro, *The Kohler Strike: Union Violence and Administrative Law* (Chicago: Henry Regnery Co., 1961). Petro's *The Kingsport Strike* reported no less than 1,000 cases of violence. (New Rochelle, N.Y.: Arlington House, 1963).

8. Edward S. Mason, *Economic Concentration and the Monopoly Problem* (Cambridge: Harvard University Press, 1961).

initially be overstated, of course, so that any subsequent concessions may pass as reasonableness, or give-and-take, and to allow unions "to have something left over for the next round to catch up upon," as one union official put it.

Clearly, no general prounion legislation (to foster "equality of bargaining power") would be applicable to all the tens of thousands of separate and unique union collective-bargaining situations, or to the thousands of employers whose degrees of power and strength vary from very little to a great deal. This point needs only to be stated to expose the emptiness of the equality-of-bargaining-power folklore of the textbooks, of the union official and of his spokesmen in the legislature. The one realistic principle of collective bargaining propounded in union literature and union oral propaganda, and acted upon in bargaining, striking, and picketing is: Take labor out of competition and keep it out.

Economic power is usually monopoly power. With competition, no one person or entity has much perceptible economic power. By combination, or joint action, a price or a wage can be increased for the combined benefit of those who have concentrated their power and are acting together—legally or illegally. Under perfect competition, the individual producer—say, a wheat farmer—or a worker acting alone, cannot raise his price; he maximizes his income by increasing his output, becoming more efficient. In so doing, he increases the national income to the benefit of all.

The purpose of market power or union monopoly is to raise the income of unionists—those who remain or become employed. The increase comes at the expense of the buyers of the product or service and of the excluded workers. It reduces the Gross National Product as a whole, and it reduces employment to the extent that the excluded workers fail to find jobs.

Taking labor out of competition is the *key* union goal. The strike, the picket line, and the use of violence—actual or potential—are established tactics and strategies to attain that goal.

25

# IMPORTANCE
# OF LABOR COST

Of all costs labor cost is vastly the most important. A typical manufacturing plant's *direct* labor costs may amount to no more than 25 percent of selling price. But an analysis of the cost components of a final product—say a bag of groceries, a gallon of gasoline, a tire, a house, or an electric range—will show that some 70 to 80 percent of the selling price is attributable to labor costs.

In 1970, total national income reached $796 billion; compensation of employees reached $602 billion, or over 75 percent of the total. By the end of the second quarter of 1971, total national income had increased by $47.3 billion; compensation of employees by $37.6 billion; the income of all other claimants by less than $10 billion. Labor compensation accounted for 80 percent of the rise in this six-month period, one that was followed by the wage-price-rent freeze of August 16, 1971. This $37.6 billion rise in labor compensation exceeded by more than 50 percent the total dividend payments received by all stockholders for the full year 1970.

In short, labor gets the major share of the nation's output, year in and year out. While it is income to the workers, it is a cost to employers; and increases such as occurred in the first half of 1971 could not but have had a powerful price impact, unless they had been offset by corresponding increases in productivity. No such increases occurred. Instead, the "creeping inflation" that the Nixon administration had been trying to check by orthodox fiscal and monetary measures (see Chapter VIII) speeded up and led to the freeze.

27

George Meany, president of the AFL-CIO, had been calling for wage-and-price controls for a year or more, provided they applied across the board. Yet when President Nixon announced the freeze, Meany, and leaders of other major unions, threatened to block the controls via law suits, strikes, contract terminations, and a host of other extralegal and illegal steps.

They apparently cannot, or will not, see that with labor getting the lion's share of the national income, the increase in money wages gained through annual collective bargaining makes price stability impossible. Like the man in the street, they are impressed by how little each cost increase, taken separately as a product moves from one stage of production to the next, affects the final price. Each cost increase is largely a wage increase, and since a "fair" wage is always more than the prevailing wage, the duty of a union official is to get raises for his members and, at a minimum, to keep them abreast of the workers in other firms involved in the long chain of production. Indeed, if he doesn't do so, he is not likely to remain their leader for long. Until the general public, including the rank and file of union workers, comes to understand certain elementary economic principles, a union official urging moderation runs a risk equal to that of a political candidate who urges a policy that runs squarely against the wishes of the majority of his constituents. This parallel merits, and indeed requires, much greater emphasis.

A tree that will yield one-thousand board feet of lumber may sell for one or two dollars. Heavy labor costs are involved in cutting down the tree, hauling it to a sawmill, and converting it into boards and other lumber. The equipment and machines used in this process, as well as the oil and gasoline or other fuel used, also have a heavy labor-cost component; and the operation of the machinery and equipment adds still more labor costs. As the lumber is hauled—say, to a furniture factory—again, the labor cost is high. The lumber may require dressing, sorting, and selecting—again, more labor costs. As the lumber is fashioned into chairs, tables, bureaus, dressers, etc., and is stained and varnished, the labor-cost component escalates. The furniture must be sold via manpower at the factory, then hauled to wholesale or retail stores, where manpower sells it to the ultimate consumer. Finally, it must be delivered to the buyer, with heavy

28

trucking costs. It is not surprising that, typically, 75 percent of product costs are labor costs.

Annual depreciation charges on investments or maintenance costs, are ultimately reducible primarily to labor costs. Most tax revenues find their way into direct and indirect labor income. True, interest costs are largely nonlabor costs, but assembling loan funds and lending money do require considerable administrative, clerical, and other similar salaried personnel.

For some reason, never clearly explained, the average person has a grossly exaggerated notion of the percentage of profits in the sales dollar. A recent survey by Opinion Research Corporation asked: "Just as a rough guess, what percent profit on each dollar of sales do you think the average manufacturer makes, after taxes?" The average guess was 28 cents, whereas the actual figure is under 5 cents. The average woman guessed 34 cents, and a special sample of teenagers guessed 33 cents. Even shareholders guessed 23 cents. Persons with incomes over $15,000 and farmers tied for the lowest guess of 21 cents—still more than 300 percent in excess of the actual average as reported by the Federal Trade Commission and the Securities and Exchange Commission.[1]

Needless to say, there is nothing wrong *per se* with workers getting a larger part of the final output of production than do those supplying the finances, the managerial direction, and the risk-taking. Without their labor—skilled, semiskilled, unskilled, professional, technical, and other—neither goods nor services would be available in their present abundance. From the days of Adam Smith down to the present, economists have recognized that competition must drive real wages to ever higher levels in societies in which saving and investing outstrip the growth of the labor force. For the West, at least, where population growth is no longer explosive, the doctrine of pre-Adam Smith times no longer holds. ("For a society to be prosperous, there must be slaves," Aristotle told us. And in Western Europe, right down to the middle of the eighteenth century, statesmen accepted as a self-evident truth the dictum: "To make a society happy, it is necessary that great numbers should be wretched as well as poor.")

---

1. *Business Week,* 18 December 1971, p. 26.

*The Wealth of Nations* (1776) marked a change in economic thinking as revolutionary as the changes in methods of production that would shortly transform a tiny island country into an empire on which the sun never set. How different was Smith's optimism from the pessimism of all the preceding centuries! "Where wages are high . . . we shall always find the workman more active, diligent and expeditious than where they are low; in England, for example, more than in Scotland; in the neighborhood of great towns more than in remote country places." Smith's rejection of monopoly and his praise of competition grew out of his conviction that the result would be to drive wages not down but up, and with them the well-being of the nation as a whole.

## EXCHANGE VIABILITY

It is also important that wages should not be determined by government fiat or by a bargaining process that raises them above the *competitive* level. Practitioners of a given trade or skill, or members of a given group can short-circuit competition only by reducing output and employment and driving the workers excluded into other lower-paying lines of work. The viability of the whole economy is thus reduced, and the balance and equilibrium essential to its smooth functioning are destroyed.

Neither political fiat nor private market power can produce the necessary balance. It comes from the interplay of innumerable and constantly changing market forces. A government that permits private groups to hold such power is soon forced to choose between inflation and some form of price freeze, and the interim before the choice has to be made is much shorter when the power is exercised by labor than when it comes from management.

There are a number of reasons why business monopoly, objectionable as it is and important as it is that it should be restrained, constitutes less of a threat to the free-enterprise system than labor monopoly. The first is that the wage component is much larger than the nonlabor component. A small increase in the latter has a minimal immediate effect; there is time to effect a cure. The second reason is

30

that the pressure from labor is continuous, while that from business is, to quote Gottfried Haberler, "a one-shot affair." And wages, unlike prices and profit margins, have only a single directional flexibility—upward.

Under an economy of highly specialized industries and workers—each producing virtually nothing for its own utility but relying on the salability of the total output—balance and equilibrium are of the utmost importance. A free market will automatically tend to find equilibrium between costs and prices and thereby maximize output and human well-being.

But market power, whether in industry or product markets or in service and labor markets, reduces exchangeability, marketability, and viability. Such power may overprice in the international markets and may in time precipitate a devaluation of the currency—a humility suffered by the United States in 1971, when we suffered the first foreign trade deficit in this century.

Thus the crux of the importance of labor cost is this viability. And it is something a society can lose, as in the United Kingdom, with almost no one being aware of what is holding down productivity and causing the standard of living to stagnate or even decline. (The plight of the United Kingdom is discussed at the close of the next chapter.)

Inflation, primarily a monetary phenomenon, is accentuated by union pressures and collective bargaining. Rising inflation-expectations powerfully affect economic and financial decision-making by savers, investors, speculators, developers, entrepreneurs, governments, and union leaders. Aggressive steps are taken wherever possible to protect against the ravages of the deterioration of the dollar.

Our concern in this study, however, goes beyond the problems of inflation. We are equally concerned with uneconomic work practices, featherbedding, the misallocation of resources, economic distortions, and underoptimal output. Short-run union interests, however understandable, seriously impair the effective operation of the economy—as do the short-run interests of business monopolies. Both run counter to the long-run interest of the individual citizen, the worker, the saver, the consumer, and the voter.

It is important to act before the malaise becomes fatal. Prof. Simons warned us a generation ago that the potential of labor unions

31

for controlling production is "the rock on which our present system is most likely to crack up." This dire warning came from a noted scholar who had no special interests to plead for. Have we the wit to heed it?

While workers appear to be working *for* employers, they are, in fact, largely working for one another. Under a private-property, enterprise system, the employer is an innovator, coordinator, and manager. He performs the key function of satisfying the multitudinous wants and desires of the free-choice consumers, most of whom are employees. They get most of the dollars that keep the system operating. Every misuse or waste of human effort and skill or other resource primarily hurts other workers, for they consume the bulk of what is produced.

Everyone's income is a cost to others. Anyone's increase in income is a rise in the cost to others, unless it is offset by a proportionate rise in productivity. A rise in output that is in line only with the rise in population places the average man and average family on a treadmill, with no rise in real income.[2]

Productivity, an engineering concept, measures the ratio between inputs—man-hours, electric energy, and capital—and outputs—food, clothing, appliances, and building materials, etc. As productivity rises there is more to share among all the income claimants; thus, the worker, the employee, the union member, has a huge stake in the efficiency of our economic system. The long-run interests of workers, as among themselves, and as between them and employers, are essentially harmonious, not antagonistic. The common interests outweigh those that conflict. But until the key importance of labor costs is fully grasped by workers, and by opinion and thought leaders, we, as voters, can hardly be expected to strip organized labor of the formidable power it possesses.

Our unwillingness to do so is all the greater because of another popular misunderstanding: the myth that the inflation now plaguing the country has denied workers the gains that collective bargaining was supposed to give them.

---

2. For a simplified explanation of these basic principles in a free society see, Warren T. Hackett and Emerson P. Schmidt, *How We Prosper Under Freedom*, 3rd ed. (Oak Brook, Ill.: Citizens Evaluation Institute, 1971).

# THE WAGE-LAG MYTH

An informal public-opinion survey in 1971-72 disclosed that more than 90 percent of the respondents, chosen from among heads of households or their spouses, believed that in the previous year consumer-price increases had exceeded the average increases in wages and salaries. But official data from government bureaus show that this widespread impression is in error. How can an overwhelming majority of people be so wrong?

Prices entering the household budget are constantly changing, some rising, some falling. The increases almost invariably attract more attention and produce more conversation than the declines. Indeed, since 1940, the CPI, assembled by the Bureau of Labor Statistics (BLS) of the U.S. Department of Labor, has declined in only two years—1949 and 1955.

Few working individuals and families get an income increase more than once a year, yet they encounter some price increase every week, or oftener. Even though shoppers follow "sales" events in local stores, these local happenings seem to be overshadowed by the steady monthly announcements by the news media of the rise in the CPI.

In an inflationary era, such as the one we live in, it would be indeed surprising if most wage earners were not convinced that rising prices were constantly wiping out their wage gains, i.e., that there is a wage lag; yet for most employees the lag does not exist.

Professors Armen A. Alchian and William R. Allen, in one of the most widely used college textbooks in economics, engaged this conundrum under a heading: "The Wage-Lag Doctrine: An Exercise in Debunking." Even in regard to inflation, they point out, one of the most common fallacies is that wage rates typically, if not always, lag behind prices; exhaustive examination of available and cited historical evidence lends no support to that contention, the authors conclude.[1]

The wage-lag bugaboo is also encouraged by the way in which the national government reports changes in prices and wages. The changes in retail prices, which most concern householders, are reported monthly in the form of the CPI. This generally appears on page one of the newspaper, and is often the first item mentioned on half-hour radio and TV newscasts.

For a brief period in the 1950s, the BLS reported price-and-wage changes at the same time *in the same news release.* This did much to calm the hurt feelings among householders. But this sensible practice was not pleasing to certain key union officials and government staffers, so it was dropped. The wage-lag myth finally deepened to the point where it took in leaders of opinion from the president of the United States, to members of the cabinet, politicians, union officials, and the public generally.[2] Union officials naturally have no reason to challenge the myth, since it supports their contention that their members are the chief victims of inflation.

Other government officials, government publications, the trade-union press, and other news and information media flood the public's brain with incomplete data, and, more seriously, with false and misleading figures and interpretations. Let us examine an instance of the latter.

---

1. Alchian and Allen, *University Economics* (Belmont, California: The Wadsworth Publishing Company, 1964 ed.) p. 725.

2. In addressing the AFL-CIO convention in Florida on 19 November 1971, the president of the United States said, "But do you know that from 1965 to 1969 when American labor was getting some of its most substantial wage increases, for most American workers in that period price increases completely ate up the wage increases." Yet, for this period BLS figures show that average hourly earnings in private nonagricultural industries increased 50 percent faster than the CPI. See, *Economic Report of the President,* 1972, p. 229.

## MAPI CORRECTS BLS DATA INTERPRETATIONS

The Bureau of Labor Statistics regularly publishes data on average weekly earnings of all nonsupervisory production workers with three dependents both in current and in constant dollars; the figures are reported both *before* deducting income and social security taxes and *after* their deduction; the latter figure showed an alleged actual decline in *real spendable* earnings in the period 1964 to December 1970. Secretary of Labor George P. Shultz, monthly bank bulletins, and many well-intentioned commentators, widely lamented this very poor showing. Shultz could see little need for union restraint right up to August 15, 1971.

The Machinery and Allied Products Institute (MAPI) went behind the gloomy government data and came up with corrected information.[3] Professor Sar Levitan and Robert Taggart III of the George Washington University independently made similar corrections.[4]

MAPI, with its customary skilled analysis and objectivity, found that the apparent sluggishness after 1964 of the wage increases of nonsupervisory production workers was due largely if not entirely to the massive influx into the labor market of youngsters and women—in response to the overfull employment conditions in the last half of the 1960s. Their pay rates and length of workweeks, distinctly below the average, pulled down the overall average pay for all workers. The labor force, thus diluted with relatively new, inexperienced personnel *appeared* to be just holding its own against inflation. But what a distressing misinterpretation of data! Incidentally, why should wage changes be calculated *after* deducting income and social security taxes? Should employees be excused from bearing their share of the cost of government?

Between 1965 and 1970, the increase in female workers was 19.9 percent, or some 3½ times as great as the increase in male workers. During this same period, the increase in the number of male workers

---

3. "Trends in Real Spendable Earnings: 'Correcting the Record,' " *Capital Goods Review*, March 1971.

4. See, *U. S. News and World Report*, 10 May 1971, and Levitan and Taggart, *Blue Collar Workers* (New York: McGraw-Hill Book Co., 1971).

aged 16-24 rose by over 15 percent, while the number of male workers aged 25 or over increased by less than 4 percent.

Data on the length of the workweek of youngsters and of women show that they tend, on the whole, to work fewer hours per week. For example, while only 2.8 percent of male employees aged 25 or over worked on a *voluntary part-time* basis in 1970, the percentage was 19.6 for all women aged 18 and over, and 22 percent for males aged 16-24. The shorter workweeks for these youngsters and women reduced the average income of all workers, and made it appear that employees' income generally lagged behind the CPI. That women and youngsters commonly receive lower pay than experienced male adult workers is so well known that it needs no further documentation here.

MAPI noted that the BLS, in describing the wage-data series, did not misrepresent it, but "the fact remains that the series is subject to wide misrepresentation." It has been used to support the demands of union officials for massive wage and wage-supplement increases in the face of shrinking profits and rising unemployment on the grounds that the workers remaining employed have received no increase in real living scales for six long years.

This is a massive distortion of the relation between the increases in the cost of living and of the earnings of typical full-time adult male workers, as well as, of course, many adult females and youngsters with a firm attachment to the labor market.

Even cabinet officers and their subalterns in the government repeatedly aired these misconceptions. Union officials on a wide front, understandably, voiced the same errors. Harry Bridges, president of the West Coast Dock Workers, supported Nixon's fight against inflation in 1971, yet said, ". . . but it is wrong to pick on the workers, who suffer first and the most from inflation." (*Time* Magazine, 30 August 1971, p. 6.) But one government source corrected the BLS impressions.

The U.S. Bureau of the Census in *Consumer Income* (Series P-60, No. 73, 30 September 1970) stated:

> During the past decade, the median earnings *(in constant dollars)* of white married men in blue-collar jobs (crafts-

36

men and operatives) increased by 25 percent. This gain was about the same as that received by white married men in other occupations, but considerably less than the gain received by married men who were Negroes or members of other races, whose median earnings rose 60 percent overall and 42 percent for craftsmen and operatives. Most of the gains by white men employed as craftsmen and operatives were received since 1965.

Responsible editors, authors, and researchers have tried to set the record straight; their failures provide no great assurance that truth will now easily win against falsehood and error.[5]


## THE 1960s

Let us now take a look at the decade of the 1960s as a whole. Gross average hourly earnings in manufacturing increased from $2.26 in 1960 to $3.36 in 1970, a rise of 49 percent; *adjusted* average hourly earnings ("adjusted" here meaning that overtime and inter-industry shifts were eliminated) jumped from 81.2 in 1960 (1967 = 100) to 119.4 in 1970, a rise of 47 percent. In this same period, the CPI increased by 31 percent. Average hourly earnings clearly did not lag behind the CPI; furthermore, these hourly figures are similar to the unrefined figures to which MAPI objected. Were the adjusted figures used (eliminating the earnings of youngsters and females who flooded into the labor market in the last half of the 1960s) the real improvement in the scale of living of the adult male worker in the 1960s would be even more marked than these figures indicate.

From 1964 to 1970, the average hourly earnings (both adjusted and unadjusted) increased by 33 percent, while the CPI rose 25 percent. Again the workers were ahead; they had not lost out as Secretary Shultz and other commentators said they had. These

---

5. An excellent example is, *Inflation, Unions and Wage Policy* (Washington: Chamber of Commerce of the United States, 1960).

figures support the findings of the Bureau of the Census cited previously.

Since the end of World War II (1945), the CPI declined only in 1949 and 1955, as noted above. The sharp rise after the mid-1960s is shown in the accompanying chart (Chart I).[6]

Under the pressures of "guns and butter too" in the 1960s, the unemployment rate dropped from a peak of 6.7 percent of the civilian labor force in 1961 (averaging 7.4 percent in the first seven months) to 3.5 percent in 1969, after which it increased again to over 6 percent in late 1970 and averaged 5.9 percent in 1971.

As unemployment dropped after 1964, increases in labor compensation mounted as shown below (Chart 2).

Despite the sharp increases in unemployment after 1969, shown by the bars on the left side of the chart, increases in hourly compensation continued upward, more than 7 percent yearly. Construction workers, teamsters, and other militant groups wrested increases double, and more than double, the national average.

The sharp rise in unemployment and in hourly compensation ran counter to the normal historic experience. Economic slack formerly brought about more moderate compensation increases or none, and prices soon declined, or rose very little. But the militancy and political power of union officials enabled negotiators to exact large increases in wages, despite rising unemployment; hence the Nixon wage-price freeze.

These massive increases were made in the late 1960s, and in 1970 and 1971, at a time when output per man-hour was slipping. The chart below shows the decline in productivity after 1966.

For the entire period from 1961 to 1965, the CPI increased under 5 percent and wage increases were by and large in line with the improvements in productivity; so these increases kept prices from falling, but they did not push the CPI up very rapidly.

---

6. Charts in this chapter and some of the analyses are used here with the permission of Dr. Frank E. Highton, based on his address to American Management Association, June 1971.

## CHART 1
### CONSUMER PRICE INDEX
### 1940-1970

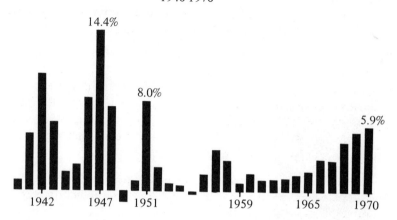

## CHART 2

**DESPITE SHARP
INCREASES IN
UNEMPLOYMENT**

**INCREASES IN
COMPENSATION
CONTINUE HIGH**

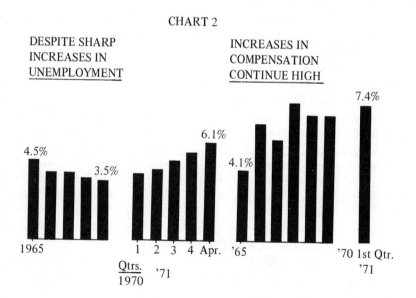

39

CHART 3
WHAT'S BEEN HAPPENING TO PRODUCTIVITY?
ANNUAL AVERAGE % INCREASE
PRIVATE SECTOR

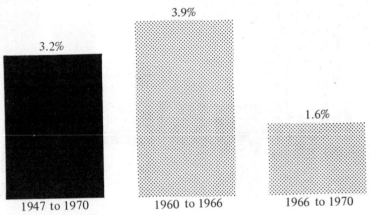

| 3.2% | 3.9% | 1.6% |
| --- | --- | --- |
| 1947 to 1970 | 1960 to 1966 | 1966 to 1970 |

Over the years, the productivity of our economy has increased at about 3 percent per annum, varying from a minus figure in 1945 to as high as plus 8.3 percent in 1950. Since we are moving more and more into a service economy, it may be more difficult to maintain this figure. The record of 1966 to 1970 (1.6 percent) is not good, as shown by the chart above.

While any increase in productivity may help to protect the devalued dollar in international markets and the domestic purchasing power of our currency, what is primarily needed is a sharp drop in the excessive annual compensation increases. At best, it appears that the rise in productivity cannot average more than 3 percent annually.

Up to the wage freeze, union-wage gains were still speeding up in 1971, as shown below (Chart 4).

The 29.6 cent increase in hourly wages shown by the bar on the right for the first quarter of 1971 compares with 22.7 cents in 1970

CHART 4

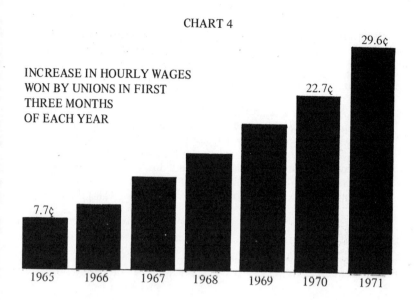

INCREASE IN HOURLY WAGES
WON BY UNIONS IN FIRST
THREE MONTHS
OF EACH YEAR

29.6¢

22.7¢

7.7¢

1965    1966    1967    1968    1969    1970    1971

and 7.7 cents in 1965. The 29.6 cents is the median—the center point in the range of 638 agreements negotiated during the first three months of 1971, based on a study of the Bureau of National Affairs. Construction led the spiral parade, with building-trade unions getting a median increase of 82.2 cents an hour, 12.7 cents higher than a year earlier. Obviously, the Nixon "game plan" to control inflation and expand the economy was not working very well; hence the midnight freeze.

The urgent need is to break the inflation-expectations. I. W. Abel, president of the steelworkers' union, said in 1971 that top priority would go to a cost-of-living escalator, and that it was a strike issue. But Heath Larry, vice president of the United States Steel Corporation, and chairman of the steel companies' bargaining team, a close student of labor economics, said that cost-of-living clauses build a spiral of inflation into the economy. Yet rising prices represent an

41

attempt to boil inflation, so to speak, as excess purchasing power, out of the economy. If the unions reinject it into the economy via escalator clauses, they and the employers who sign the clauses are assuring either more inflation or more unemployment, or some of both.

In spite of his critical reaction to the freeze, George Meany had voiced sound doctrine when he said in 1945:

> The American Federation of Labor has never agreed to the principle of basing wages on cost of living or on price inflation. The established wage policy of this country has always been based on raising wages as increases in productivity made this possible. This is the only possible basis for an expanding economy with rising living standards. (George Meany, *War Labor Reports,* 1945.)

Raising money wages is not the only way to share productivity gains, and probably not the best way. That labor and all other consumers can share only what is produced is so obvious that one is almost ashamed to repeat it. Yet spokesmen for powerful special-

CHART 5

OUTPUT PER MAN-HOUR AND REAL COMPENSATION
PER MAN-HOUR, TOTAL PRIVATE ECONOMY, 1950-69

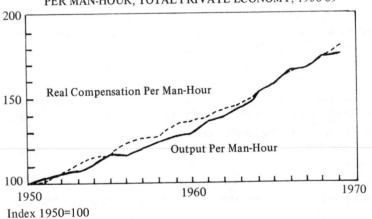

Index 1950=100

interest groups seem unable to grasp this simple truth. The soundness of Meany's 1945 statement—that increases in productivity are what make wage increases possible—is illustrated by the accompanying chart (Chart 5).

Note the very close connection over a period of twenty years between the rise in *real* compensation per man-hour and the output per man-hour. Or, to put the relationship in another way: when the rise in hourly *money* wages is deflated by the rise in prices, the rise in *real* hourly compensation parallels the rise in output per man-hour. Thus, as Dr. Frank E. Highton has put it, "It may be said that hourly compensation increases in excess of output per man-hour are paid for, as the late Walter Reuther put it, in the wooden nickels of inflation."

Even if productivity rises (measured in output per hour), the gain may take the form of reduced hours per week, more paid holidays, more absenteeism, etc. Productivity is better measured on a man-year rather than a man-hour basis. Even so, rising unit costs of inputs may vitiate the gain from productivity. On the argument that more productivity is the answer to inflation, G. M. Brannon then of the U.S. Treasury has pointed out:

> This may be true to an extent, but is not self-evident. . . .
> If productivity gains go into higher money wage rates . . .
> there will be no particular gain on inflation from this
> source.

The emphasis on higher productivity is valid and urgent; but too often warnings such as Brannon's are completely overlooked.[7]

Before Phase I of the wage-price freeze of 1971 ended, the president appointed a cabinet-level cost-of-living council, a tripartite pay board, and a price commission. The Pay Board announced a target ceiling for annual wage and salary increases of 5.5 percent; the Price Commission a target of only 2.5 percent, less than half the projected rise in compensation for employees. The aim, the public

---

7. See Brannon, "Tax Incentives for Increased Productivity," *Business Economics* (Washington: National Association of Business Economists, January 1971).

was informed, was to reduce inflation to 2 or 3 percent by the end of 1972. The expected rise in productivity of around 3 percent, plus the 2.5 percent rise in prices (midway point of the expected inflation for 1972), would allow wages and salaries to rise by 5.5 percent. Thus, *the wage-lag myth was once again exploded—at least as indicated by government plans under Phase II of the new "incomes policies" launched after Phase I of the freeze.*

Union officials and other union spokesmen face a rather embarrassing dilemma. Union members must devoutly believe that the union raises wages and brings countless other benefits, but it is equally important that the general public believe that wage increases do not cause higher prices.

When prices do rise, unionists typically blame the increase on rising profits. But profits, as economists define the term, are a residual, and tend to affect costs only after a considerable delay. What economists label as "normal profits"—the reward and incentive needed to hold resources in their current uses—are costs. These are, however, too minute to affect prices materially. More important, they do not rise year after year, decade after decade, and hence cannot cause the constant inflation that union officials and some politicians invoke as the justification for wage increases.

Although union officials and politicians of both major parties had urged wage-price controls for some years, during the freeze and its sequels, union officials and opposition-party politicians labeled the economic stabilization program a sham, a program for big business, a penalty on labor and unions, a design to raise profits, etc. In a great huff, the AFL-CIO members of the Pay Board resigned on March 23, 1972. The board was quickly reconstituted as an all-public-member agency by President Nixon, with one union man and one businessman serving with five other persons.

Government efforts were then made to show the changes in the CPI and in wages *in the same release.* For example, the Cost-of-Living Council in its *Economic Stabilization Quarterly Report* (January-March 1972) carried a table showing *on a single page* (page 73) wage and CPI changes from August 1970 through March 1972 for five different time spans; in every case money wages increased more rapidly than the CPI, except for one three-month period, showing a

rise in real earnings. Note particularly the *1967 dollar* figures showing the rise in real income on the next two pages.

Much of what appears in union newspapers, leaflets, pamphlets,
etc., is designed to "prove" that collectively bargained wage increases
have no price effects. Thus, in January 1960, in *Labor's Economic
Review,* the AFL-CIO stated:

> The evidence shows that wage settlements in the postwar
> period have generally been in line with changes in the price
> level and changes in the productivity of the economy.

Actually, the statement would have been more nearly correct, if it
had hypothetically read:

> The evidence shows that wage settlements in the postwar
> period have *been more than twice the rise in the price level
> and wage settlements have been about twice the rise in
> productivity.*

In *Memo from Cope* (the AFL-CIO political-action bulletin) of
January 17, 1972, a series of stirring, graphic charts, graphs, photos,
and words lament the rise in the cost of living (incidentally, a figure
miscalculated) without any recognition of the more than parallel rise
in wages.

There has been little improvement in the quality of the economic
analysis in union literature, or even in the general newspaper and
other periodical literature, despite the rising level of the schooling of
the average union member. But the longer the wage-lag myth flour-
ishes, the greater will be the apparent need for more unionism and
more militant leadership. The rank and file will not peer behind the
figures and come up with a myth-free notion of the relations between living costs, productivity, and hourly or weekly wages. A
feeling of being underpaid seems to be shared by all of us; if we also
conclude that the things we buy rise more rapidly in price than our
labor does, our feelings of injury or injustice are accentuated.

The combined pressures of union demands, government over-
spending and deficiteering, foreign involvement, and the policy of
overfull employment were enough to precipitate the 1971 crisis. The
plight of the dollar in international markets was the immediate cause

Average Hourly Earnings and Real Weekly Earnings,
Gross and Spendable* Percentage Changes at
Annual Rates, Seasonally Adjusted

| | 12 months 8/70-8/71 | 7 months 1/71-8/71 | 7 months 8/71-3/72 | 3 months 8/71-11/71 | 4 months 11/71-3/72 |
|---|---|---|---|---|---|
| **Average Hourly Earnings** | | | | | |
| Private Nonfarm | 6.1 | 6.8 | 6.0 | 2.3 | 8.9 |
| 1967 $ | 1.4 | 2.5 | 3.7 | 1.4 | 5.4 |
| Manufacturing | 5.6 | 5.5 | 7.4 | 1.1 | 12.1 |
| 1967 $ | 1.0 | 1.2 | 4.1 | 0.0 | 7.3 |
| **Adjusted Hourly Earnings\*\*** | | | | | |
| Private Nonfarm | 6.9 | 6.8 | 6.1 | 1.9 | 9.3 |
| 1967 $ | 2.3 | 2.8 | 3.1 | 0.3 | 5.3 |

Adjusted Hourly Earnings**

| | | | | | |
|---|---|---|---|---|---|
| Manufacturing | 6.5 | 6.2 | 6.1 | 0.7 | 10.5 |
| 1967 $ | 2.0 | 2.2 | 3.2 | -1.0 | 6.7 |
| Gross Weekly Earnings | 5.6 | 6.8 | 7.0 | 4.6 | 8.9 |
| 1967 $ | 1.1 | 2.8 | 4.1 | 2.9 | 5.0 |
| Spendable Weekly Earnings*** | 6.5 | 5.0 | 8.9 | 4.1 | 12.6 |
| 1967 $ | 2.0 | 2.0 | 5.9 | 2.4 | 8.7 |
| Consumer Price Index | 4.4 | 3.9 | 2.8 | 1.7 | 3.7 |

*For Production or Nonsupervisory Workers.

**Adjusted for Overtime Hours (Manufacturing Only) and Interindustry Shifts in Employment.

***For a Worker with Three Dependents.

of the dramatic action taken by President Nixon. A dollar crisis in the spring of 1971 had been patched over.[8] By the summer of that year, foreign governments had accumulated great quantities of surplus dollars. On a single day, the central bank of Germany acquired over one billion dollars. On August 13, the Bank of England requested the United States to guarantee against devaluation of its dollar holdings, then totaling some $3 billion. The Japanese yen was likewise grossly undervalued relative to our dollar, and finally, on August 28th, Japan let the yen float—that is, it devalued our overvalued dollar.

We still have the largest and possibly the strongest economy in the world. But it has slipped, and will slip more, unless we put our monetary and fiscal affairs in order and disperse private monopoly power, particularly union power. We must find some way to restore competition in the labor market—as we did in the goods market through antitrust laws—sparking internal competition, tariff reductions, and in other ways. Time is of the essence, as United Kingdom experience should warn us.


## WARNING: THE U. K. DECLINE

In the early phase of the Industrial Revolution of the eighteenth century, England became the "workshop of the world," with the highest per capita income of all nations, a position it held for about 150 years. World peace, and economic progress elsewhere, depended heavily on this once great country. We owe much else to this land and its people.

But a plethora of disabilities seemed to overtake her in the twentieth century. More or less chronic mismanagement of monetary affairs had been reflected in frequent imbalance in international payments, often called "the British disease." England virtually moved to the sidelines as a peacemaker, even withdrawing defenses

---

8. *Newsweek,* 24 May 1971, p. 72. Dr. Milton Friedman insists that we encountered a German mark crisis, not a dollar crisis.

from what remained of her empire. This is not the place for an exhaustive treatment of the reasons for the decline of the United Kingdom[9]; yet we cannot refrain from noting a massive transformation of the attitudes and practices of a key segment of that wondrous workshop: the workmen and their unions.

The labor movement of the United Kingdom came to be possibly the most output-restriction-minded in the world, according to the evidence and sources cited by Chamberlin, Carson, and others. The hostility between management and union officials, and often union members—even when management was the state itself in the socialized sectors—possibly has no parallel in the rest of the world. "A fair day's work for a fair wage" is not a part of the Queen's English. *The Economist* pointed out that the direct and indirect effect of the union strikes, over 90 percent of which were unofficial, was to reduce the national income by a greater percentage than was suffered by other countries. In 1971 the United Kingdom adopted an industrial-relations act, limiting the powers of unions and providing penalties for certain antisocial actions.

The World Bank in its *World Bank Atlas* (1971) shows how other countries have overtaken the United Kingdom in annual per-capita GNP (an essentially similar ratio applies to national income). The United States remained at the head of the list in 1969, with a per-capita GNP of $4,240, in contrast to the United Kingdom figure of $1,890. Other countries exceeding the United Kingdom figure included Western Germany, France, Belgium, Sweden, Switzerland, Denmark, Norway, Luxembourg, Australia, and New Zealand. Even Finland outperformed the erstwhile workshop of the world, and Iceland fell only 2 percent below the United Kingdom. The United Kingdom's economic growth rate was the lowest in all of Europe from 1960 to 1969.

Here we see a dramatic transformation from world leadership to slowdown, weakness, and malaise. Do we have the will and the wit to learn from history?

---

9. Wm. H. Chamberlin, "The Failing Dynamo," *The Freeman*, May 1969; and see a series of articles in the same magazine on "The Rise and Fall of England" by Clarence B. Carson, beginning in March 1968.

# ANNUAL WAGE INCREASES VERSUS OTHER INCOMES

In previous chapters, the importance of the relationship of labor costs and the rapid rise of wage rates to consumer prices and productivity improvements have been noted. In this chapter a look is taken at wage trends versus other reward trends. The other income claimants—savers, investors, risk-takers, and landlords—rarely, if ever, make collective demands. They usually take what the free competitive market allocates to them.

Union officials annually (or more often, through escalator clauses) make collective demands for marking up the sales price of an hour's or a day's work. From which of these other income claimants does the union official expect to get that higher price for labor? He doesn't always say—but he does expect it, and he does get it.

Do these other income shares—profits, interest, rents, including economic rents—have anything to spare that the union official can round up and collect? Do collective bargaining, the strike, and the picket line yield anything that the normal competitive processes would not yield? For a specific union? Unions in general? Labor in general?

Some of these questions are answered here; others are discussed in later chapters. We will see here that while wage rates and salaries, with fringe benefits, rise annually in the majority of cases, the income rates of the other income claimants show no secular or long-run rise. The one exception to this generalization may be the return to the owners of fixed-supply natural resources—lands, minerals, waterfalls, and water resources generally.

Let us first look at the average annual yields of selected types of

## AVERAGE ANNUAL YIELD ON SELECTED TYPES OF INVESTMENTS—1930-1970*

| Year | Savings Accounts in Savings Associations | Savings Deposits in Mutual-Savings Banks | Time and Savings Deposits in Commercial Banks | United States Government Bonds | State and Local Bonds | Corporate (AAA) Bonds |
|---|---|---|---|---|---|---|
| 1930 | 5.3% | 4.5% | ·3.9% | 3.3% | 4.1% | 4.6% |
| 1935 | 3.1 | 2.7 | 2.6 | 2.8 | 3.4 | 3.6 |
| 1940 | 3.3 | 2.0 | 1.3 | 2.2 | 2.5 | 2.8 |
| 1945 | 2.5 | 1.7 | 0.8 | 2.4 | 1.5 | 2.6 |
| 1950 | 2.5 | 1.9 | 0.9 | 2.3 | 1.9 | 2.6 |
| 1955 | 2.9 | 2.6 | 1.4 | 2.8 | 2.6 | 3.1 |
| 1960 | 3.86 | 3.47 | 2.56 | 4.01 | 3.69 | 4.41 |
| 1965 | 4.23 | 4.11 | 3.69 | 4.21 | 3.34 | 4.49 |
| 1966 | 4.45 | 4.45 | 4.04 | 4.66 | 3.90 | 5.13 |
| 1967 | 4.67 | 4.74 | 4.24 | 4.85 | 3.99 | 5.51 |
| 1968 | 4.68 | 4.76 | 4.48 | 5.25 | 4.48 | 6.18 |
| 1969 | 4.80 | 4.85 | 4.87 | 6.10 | 5.73 | 7.03 |
| 1970 | 5.09 | 5.03 | 4.92 | 6.59 | 6.42 | 8.04 |

* *Savings-and-Loan Fact Book*, 1971, United States Savings and Loan League, Chicago.

savings or investments beginning in 1930. In 1970, as shown in the first column, the yield on savings accounts in savings associations had not quite recovered to the rate of forty years earlier. Clearly, there is no secular rise here in earnings per dollar of savings. The average annual yield on deposits in mutual savings banks (second column) shows the same long-run trend. Savings deposits in commercial banks (interest payments on demand deposits or checkbook money are illegal) show closely similar earnings rates—a very low long-run rise. Interest on savings invested in U. S. government bonds, state and local government bonds, and corporation bonds have failed to double in four decades.

Beginning in the mid-1960s, interest payments for bonds began to rise, due to inflation expectations. A bond yielding 5 percent per year when inflation is occurring at the same rate has a zero return; the decline in purchasing power of the principal fully offsets the interest yield. Historical experience covering several centuries indicates that the earnings rates for savings will probably return to something like the long-run rates shown in the following table, if inflation expectations subside.

The net rate of interest earned on invested funds of the life-insurance companies has shown no upward trend, as the table below shows. The rate of return for 1965 was actually lower than the first year shown, fifty years earlier.[1]

## NET EARNINGS OF LIFE INSURANCE FUNDS

| Year | Rate |
|------|------|
| 1915 | 4.77% |
| 1920 | 4.83 |
| 1930 | 5.05 |
| 1940 | 3.45 |
| 1950 | 3.13 |
| 1960 | 4.11 |
| 1965 | 4.61 |
| 1970 | 5.30 |

1. *1971 Life Insurance Fact Book* (New York: Institute of Life Insurance, 971).

Interest rates charged for personal credit at banks and other loan institutions show no rising trend. Apparently the market does not provide these savers and investors with annual rate increases. Net rentals for residential properties, office space, etc., similarly show no rising trend since 1900 (after allowing for higher operating costs, including property taxes).

Should labor get annual compensation increases while millions of thrifty persons who more or less regularly save and invest parts of their income are denied such benign treatment? Apparently, the answer lies in the fundamental supply-and-demand conditions of the two markets, the labor markets and the capital markets.

## INTEREST

Many, possibly most, people live from hand to mouth, having no systematic savings plans and rarely bothering to set aside any voluntary savings (except possibly by going into debt and getting out over-time—a form of saving in most cases). But many people are conditioned to save, some of them even at a zero interest rate. Savings take many forms: buying securities, taking mortgages, making deposits in banks and other institutions, buying life insurance, buying land or other real estate. Over the centuries the basic premium for savings, the interest rate, during periods of calm and relatively stable prices (noninflation), has averaged about 3 percent. Rates above that figure in specific markets are due to differential administration costs and risks, inflationary prospects, or temporary surges in demand for capital. Even though basic long-run trends shift little, interest rates paid in the innumerable demand-supply markets of funds may differ widely from one another.

Evidently a fairly stable rate of interest suffices to bring forth the savings people are prepared to make for the better future most of them clearly want. The rate produces a balance between saving and investing: the amounts people will voluntarily save and the amounts they, or others, can profitably invest. The interest reward serves a very essential and useful purpose. Yet, modest as the rate has been over long periods of time, savers are popularly held in low esteem.

John Maynard Keynes, on numerous occasions, urged the end, the disappearance, "the euthanasia of the rentier" and the "functionless investor."[2] Keynes's prediction of the probable demand for capital proved grossly in error. But other critics, too, take extreme positions on the roles of savings and savers in our society. Wider understanding of the remarkable stability of interest-rate returns may remove one source of social friction. And persistent inflation, whether wage-push or not, will force interest rates upward, to correct for the dollar depreciation. Lenders will not willingly see their capital vanish in the swirl of inflation.

## PROFITS

Business profits, both as a return on shareholders' equity and per-dollar of sales, also fail to show any long-run increase. They are decidedly the most volatile component of our national income, rising in times of boom and falling when economic slack occurs, and varying enormously among the millions of enterprises and for individual firms from time to time. That is why winners in the stock market are hard to pick in advance.

Profit expectations play a powerful role in the plans of production units—proprietorships, partnerships, or corporations. Although accountants and income-tax collectors tend to view profits as a surplus over costs of doing business, economists take a more complicated view of them.

To begin with, some part of profits, the part frequently referred to as normal profits, are a cost. A person's own savings used in his own business (equity capital) might instead have been lent at, say, 5 percent per annum. That part of what may appear to the accountant as profit is actually "implicit" interest. Only earnings in excess of implicit interest should properly be called profits—the reward for successful enterprising and risk-taking.

---

2. J. M. Keynes, *The General Theory of Employment Interest and Money* New York: Harcourt, Brace and Company, 1936), p. 376 passim. For a more careful exposition of the phenomenon of interest see a standard economics text book, such as *University Economics*, already cited.

A firm aiming to maximize true profits will tend to expand production to the point at which the last dollar invested will yield no additional net revenue. A farmer, for example, will try to equalize the added cost of applying one more dollar's worth of fertilizer by adding to his total revenue with an increase in output. (In the technical jargon of economics, he strives to equalize marginal cost with marginal revenue. Going beyond or stopping short of that point means that his profit is less than it otherwise would have been.)

What applies to the single farmer applies equally to business, large and small; to a monopolist quite as much as to the firm under rigorous competition. At this equilibrium point, there is neither profit nor loss on the last dollar invested. The monopolist, of course, will make monopoly profits on his entire investment. The competitive firm will be making only implicit interest, which it must receive to justify staying in business; thus competition tends to whittle away excess profits—those that do not enter into costs.

The profit dynamic helps to make our economic system adapt to consumer demands and changing consumer needs, tastes, and desires. The firm failing to make a profit may disappear or be absorbed by a more successful enterprise. As this happens, human and other re-·sources are released and put to uses more highly valued by consumers. If competition is pervasive, the rivalry among producers (wholesalers, retailers, financial institutions—all are producers) constantly tends to lower relative prices to the point where profits above those defined as "normal" approach zero. If profits—that is, earnings above the implicit-interest return—actually do tend to disappear and become zero, or even a minus quantity, why would anyone launch a new business? Why would anyone buy stock in a corporation? Why put savings for old age and a rainy day into corporate equities? Is there still something missing?

Here we must concern ourselves with human nature and its infinite variations. Most people apparently prefer to find their way onto someone else's payroll; a few prefer to be self-employed, or to become job givers, employers, entrepreneurs. These are usually individuals who have considerable self-confidence, imagination, enterprise, and inventive and innovative ability. They see, or think they see, a chance to make more than a good wage or salary—their aim is profits. They may have a patent, or a new idea. They may have some funds and enough credit among friends or financial institutions to launch their enterprises. If their guesses, hunches, and knowledge are right, and they make the right moves and decisions, their enterprises turn out to be profitable. Success makes for more effort, more innovations, more new products or services, and lower prices. Their profits mount.

But if Mr. A can do all this, Mr. B and then Mr. C may try it out in the same industry. So long as we have freedom of entry by new enterprises, profits as here defined are vulnerable. As producers cover the field, supplies of output rise, prices come under greater downward pressures, and the weakest enterprises may quit, go bankrupt, or be absorbed by the more successful or by a conglomerate. Profits for some firms become losses, and for the survivors, they may be reduced, remain stable for a time or even rise. The outcome is always uncertain. The Pennsylvania Railroad paid a dividend for more than 100 years, but in 1970, as a part of the Penn Central Railroad, it went into receivership. Some 1,500 companies have actually produced automobiles in the United States in this century; about half a dozen have survived. Very few companies listed on the New York stock exchange in 1900 are listed there now.

In most industries, individual enterprises range from the highly profitable to the disastrous. Labor-union bargainers virtually always argue that higher employee compensation can come out of profits and will hence have no price effects. This "ability-to-pay" argument has great popular appeal, since profits are suspect. Tapping them to enrich workers obviously benefits the workers and raises the standing of union officials; and the consumer doesn't in any way pay for it! Once the "industry leader," the highly profitable one, has agreed to the union demands, possibly after a strike, union officials generally invoke the "equal-pay-for-equal-work" slogan and demand that other companies in the industry accept the same terms.

In this fashion, the union converts profits into enduring labor costs, and the *consumer* does pay. To explain how the profitability among members of an industry varies from high to low to zero or minus, economists employ what they call an entrepreneurial-differential-cost curve, as shown in a highly simplified chart.

## CHART 6
### ENTREPRENEURIAL DIFFERENTIAL COSTS

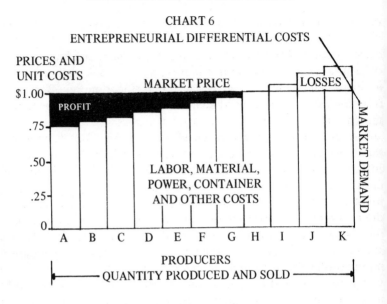

If all the companies in a given industry are arranged on a chart, with the lowest-cost producers at the left, the peaks of the bars suggest three different costs of the different companies. The companies may all make an identical product, say carbon steel, which sells at a fairly uniform price. The chart shows the demand curve for the product. (For simplicity in this illustration, it is assumed that total supply is given, and that all producers sell identical amounts of the product.)

The marginal producers—those with costs equal to the selling price—are just breaking even; a few companies—I, J, and K (submarginal)—are losing money; others are making profits, with a few making very large profits as a percentage of sales, or on invested capital. The larger profits of the few are the reward for superior decision-making and effective cost control. These differentials are found in all industries.

In his wage demands, the union official generally cites the profits of the most successful company, even though he expects high-cost companies to meet his demands, too; so, price effects of wage demands are inevitable—they hit marginal and high-cost producers as well as the more profitable ones. *The differential cost curve of the entire industry is raised.* The argument that wage increases come out of profits is simply fallacious.

What makes the argument plausible is the time lag in the price response. The price cannot rise until there is a decline in output, and no decline will occur until some of the producers, presumably the submarginal ones, go out of business. This does not happen overnight. So long as price covers a firm's out-of-pocket costs and leaves a little over to amortize its fixed investment in plant and equipment, closing down and selling plant and equipment as scrap frequently involves a greater loss than continuing, though at a reduced production rate. Many firms with heavy investment in specialized equipment may operate for years at a small loss to avoid a larger one. (It should be noted in passing that a wage increase imposed on a monopolist will have a more immediate price effect. The higher wage will destroy the old marginal-cost-marginal-revenue equilibrium. The new one will involve a reduction in output; hence an increase in the price consumers will have to pay for the product. Thus, even in the case of monopoly, some part of a collectively bargained wage increase is shifted to consumers.)

Given productivity improvements, higher wages also mean higher prices than would otherwise prevail. To convert temporary profits into permanent labor costs deprives the consumers of the gains of economic progress.

It is the function of competition—through product improvement, new products, expansion of existing companies, new entries, development of substitutes—to discipline the market and whittle down profits that are temporarily above normal. Despite delays and market imperfections, this process works pervasively and effectively and in ways that direct investment into the production of things the consumers want. The market works in their behalf. Converting elusive, temporary profits into labor costs is a sure way to deny the consumer what he has a right to expect from a free-market economy.

Profits are a fluctuating residual share of national income. In boom times, total profits may temporarily increase faster than other income shares, just as in a recession they fall more rapidly—and may even become losses. They are *not inflexible* as are wage costs. And when they do rise, they do not establish a higher rigid cost plateau, as higher wages do.

Moreover, profits show no rising trend over the long pull as does employee remuneration. Let us examine some data. The Standard & Poor's 500-company stocks yielded the following dividend:

## DIVIDEND YIELD OF STOCKS

| Year | Rate |
|------|------|
| 1940 | 5.59% |
| 1950 | 6.57 |
| 1960 | 3.47 |
| 1965 | 3.00 |
| 1970 | 3.83 |

Net profit per dollar of sales shows no upward trend with the passage of time. The figures for all manufacturing companies confirm this statement:

## PROFIT PER DOLLAR OF SALES IN MANUFACTURING

| Year | Durable Goods Rate | Nondurable Goods Rate |
|------|------|------|
| 1949 | 5.8% | 5.4% |
| 1950 | 7.1 | 6.5 |
| 1955 | 5.4 | 5.1 |
| 1960 | 4.4 | 4.8 |
| 1965 | 5.6 | 5.5 |
| 1970 | 3.5 | 4.5 |

These are net profit figures. If they suggest any trend at all, it is downward. It is also worth noting that the earnings shifts are similar in both the durable and the nondurable-goods sectors of our manufacturing enterprises. The figures for 1970, after five years of considerable inflation, are lower than any other figure. There is no profit escalation for savers, investors, and risk-takers; they have no general cost-of-living protection.

From 1960 to 1970, the Consumer Price Index increased by more than 30 percent; but the earnings per dollar of sales in 1970 were lower than in either 1950 or 1960.[3]

Corporate net profits were 4.2 percent of the Gross National Product in 1970. Profits declined from a peak of $49.9 billion in 1966, and were lower in absolute amount in 1970 than in any year since 1964, and lower as a share of the GNP than in any year since 1938. The contrast with wage rates and labor income would be even more striking if we corrected these figures (1) for the overall growth of the corporate sector, and (2) for the decline in the purchasing power of the corporate-dollar profit, or the dividend dollar. Yet in the 1960s, George Meany repeatedly asserted, "We have a profit inflation and nothing else." *The Evening Star* (Washington, D.C., 24 February 1969) carried this gem from Miami Beach from the executive council of the AFL-CIO: "Most essential to achievement of relative price stability is lower profit margins and reduced profit rates of return on investment."

Similar statements came from the headquarters of the federation virtually every month. Further, the member unions, their locals, and their members play constant variations on the same theme. News media always let these entirely unsupportable assertions stand without correction or follow-up questions. The accompanying table shows the relatively small share of the GNP, the national income, or the sales dollar, that corporation profits reflect. (None of these figures are corrected for the decline in the purchasing power of the dollar).

## LAND OWNERS INCLUDING FARMERS

Farmers, too, have been caught in a cost-price squeeze. From 1947 to the end of 1970, prices received by American farmers for their output showed no rise whatever; indeed, they showed a decline of

---

3. *Economic Report of the President,* 1971.

# CORPORATE PROFITS[4]

| Year or Quarter | Corporate Profits In Billions of Dollars Before Taxes | Corporate Profits In Billions of Dollars After Taxes | Corporate Profits after Taxes as percent of: GNP | National Income | Income Originating in Corporations | Corporate Gross Product* | Sales** Manufacturing Corporations |
|---|---|---|---|---|---|---|---|
| 1929 | $10.5 | $ 9.1 | 8.8% | 10.5% | 19.8% | 16.9% | n.a. |
| 1939 | 6.3 | 4.9 | 5.4 | 6.7 | 13.2 | 10.5 | n.a. |
| 1961 | 50.3 | 27.2 | 5.2 | 6.4 | 10.5 | 8.5 | 4.3 |
| 1962 | 55.7 | 31.5 | 5.6 | 6.9 | 11.3 | 9.1 | 4.6 |
| 1963 | 58.9 | 32.6 | 5.5 | 6.8 | 11.1 | 9.0 | 4.7 |
| 1964 | 66.3 | 37.9 | 6.0 | 7.3 | 11.9 | 9.6 | 5.2 |
| 1965 | 76.1 | 44.8 | 6.5 | 7.9 | 12.9 | 10.5 | 5.6 |
| 1966 | 82.4 | 48.1 | 6.6 | 7.8 | 12.7 | 10.4 | 5.6 |
| 1967 | 78.7 | 45.5 | 5.7 | 7.3 | 12.4 | 10.1 | 5.0 |
| 1968 | 84.3 | 44.5 | 5.1 | 6.2 | 11.1 | 9.0 | 5.1 |
| 1969 | 78.6 | 39.0 | 4.2 | 5.1 | 9.2 | 7.4 | 4.8 |
| 1970 | 70.8 | 36.7 | 3.8 | 4.6 | 8.5 | 6.8 | 4.0 |
| 1971 | 81.0 | 43.2 | 4.1 | 5.1 | 9.3 | 7.4 | 4.2 |

4. United States Department of Commerce, the Conference Board, *The Wall Street Journal*, 12 June 1972. Prepared by Martin R. Gainsbrugh, Vice President, The Conference Board, Inc. Reproduced with permission of CIT Financial Corp., sponsor.

Note: Profits are after inventory valuation adjustment.

* Excludes branch profits remitted from abroad net of corresponding United States remittances to foreigners.
** Cents per dollar of sales.

about 5 percent. Meantime, their operating costs—including wages paid, interest, taxes, etc.—jumped by 66 percent from 70 in 1947 (1967 = 100) to 116 by the end of 1970.

The farm-income parity ratio—a somewhat artificial formula based on relationships in the unusually prosperous period of 1910-14—stood at 115 in 1947; by the end of 1970 it stood at below 70.[5]

These declines occurred in spite of numerous efforts by Congress to shore up farm prices and incomes. Direct government payments to farmers have not changed the above trends at all since 1947.

In terms of hardship or poverty, these figures present an unduly bleak picture for two reasons. First, they fail to take account of the numbers involved. Farm population declined drastically in the last generation—from about 25 percent of total population in the 1930s, to under 5 percent by the end of 1970. In constant prices—that is, inflationary effects eliminated—income per farm *from farming* increased from $3,534 in 1947 to $4,880 in 1970; and farmers earned almost as much again, 93 percent, from ownership of nonfarm assets, off-the-farm work, social insurance, etc.

Second, the apparent decline in farmers' income is offset in part by the rise in land values. Land, being largely fixed in supply, tends to rise in value as population grows, as the GNP rises, and as interest rates drop. The value of any earning asset, such as land, is the current price, or market value to the rights to a future stream of income. But this concept involves an assumed rate of interest at which the prospective income is capitalized. The lower the general rate of interest assumed, the higher will be the present value of a given stream of income and, therefore, the asset producing that income.

Not only farmers but any owners of land or other scarce fixed-supply resources may benefit from this capitalization of future income—as the prospective flow of income is widely believed to rise. Such capital gain, many economists have argued, is not actually income. In any case, present owners may have had to pay the anticipated higher capital value when they acquired the asset; thus the seller, not the present owner, may have cashed in on the rising value, or the risen value.

5. *Economic Report of the President,* 1971, pp. 294-95.

The rising-land-value component in real property and rental income, and the rise in the value of other fixed-supply resources (minerals, waterfalls, etc.) may lead to some long-run or secular rise in asset values and, therefore, become income when the asset is sold. This condition, while not parallel to the annual rise in wage and salary incomes, is a departure from the extreme stability of interest rates and average-profit rates over long periods of time.

## COMPENSATION OF EMPLOYEES

Contrast the dreary level of profit and interest income with the upward spiraling of average hourly earnings in manufacturing or compensation per man-hour in the entire private economy as shown in the second and fourth columns in the accompanying table.

All the figures in the above table are based on 1967 = 100, in order to make for easy and careful comparisons. Hourly earnings, as well as compensation per hour in the entire private economy, have risen on average by about 200 percent since 1947. Because of technology, research, innovation, new methods, more investment per job, a minor improvement in labor quality, and superior entrepreneurship, unit-labor costs have mounted less rapidly as shown in the third column (manufacturing) and in the fifth column. Nevertheless, unit labor costs have mounted in these years since 1947. Thanks to productivity improvement, the CPI only doubled from 1929 to 1967, and has increased less rapidly since 1967 than have hourly earnings and overall compensation per man-hour in the private economy.

## QUESTIONS

Why should all income claimants in our economy, except employees and possibly self-employed persons, be subjected to a dreary, level income rate per dollar saved, invested, or risked? Why do these nonlabor income claimants have no long-fun, built-in, price-level-increase protection?

## CONSUMER PRICES, WAGE RATES, UNIT LABOR COSTS[6]
### (1967 = 100)

| Year | CPI | Average Hourly Earnings* | Unit Labor Cost* | Compensation Per Hour in Private Economy** | Unit Labor Cost in Private Economy |
|------|-----|-----|-----|-----|-----|
| 1929 | 51 | 22 | | 36 | 71 |
| 1939 | 42 | 24 | | 43 | 72 |
| 1947 | 67 | 44 | 68 | | |
| 1950 | 72 | 52 | 69 | 56 | 80 |
| 1955 | 80 | 66 | 81 | 72 | 92 |
| 1960 | 89 | 81 | 96 | 88 | 94 |
| 1965 | 94 | 92 | 93 | 94 | 96 |
| 1966 | 97 | 96 | 96 | | |
| 1967 | 100 | 100 | 100 | 100 | 100 |
| 1968 | 104 | 106 | 102 | 108 | 105 |
| 1969 | 110 | 112 | 107 | 115 | 111 |
| 1970 | 116 | 120 | 113 | 124 | 118 |

6. Ibid.
* Data in manufacturing.
** Includes employers contribution to social insurance and private benefit plans.

Has the trade union speeded up or slowed down the growth of the national income? Has it increased the proportion of this income going to labor? Have the gains of some unions been made at the expense of other workers? At the expense of savers? Risk-takers? Farmers, land and other resource owners?

Before these questions are considered, another one is in order. Is government policy, rather than union power, responsible for the income distribution reflected in this and the preceding chapter? We address this question in the next chapter. We shall find that a great change took place in the attitudes of the lawmakers toward labor and the whole issue of income distribution during the Great Depression of the 1930s. Taxing and spending were deliberately shaped to transfer income from the rich to the poor. Laws were passed to increase union power, and they succeeded to such an extent that it now rivals, if it does not surpass, that of government itself.

# UNION POWERS
# CREATED BY
# GREAT DEPRESSION
# LEGISLATION

The severity and duration of the Great Depression are now recognized by most economists to be the results of serious mistakes by the FED (the Federal Reserve System—a government agency). The Congress, while not directly responsible, approved the monetary policy of the FED and passed laws that built up the monopoly power of the unions; thus so weakening competition generally as to make a bad situation worse. The FED has unquestionably learned from its mistakes; there is little or no evidence that Congress has.

Until the depression, union bargaining functioned in a twilight zone of legality. The Sherman Antitrust Act of 1890 had been applied to unions in numerous cases. Railway strikes had been found to violate the right to move the mails.

The Clayton Act of 1914, with its declaration that "labor is not a commodity," was labeled the Magna Carta of unionism by Samuel Gompers, president of the American Federation of Labor from 1886 to 1924 in all but one year. But the courts ruled that the services provided by labor were subject to antitrust laws.

In 1927 the U. S. Supreme Court upheld an injunction against a stone-cutters' union for its boycott of the products of some firms quarrying limestone in the Bedford-Bloomington district of Indiana. The firms had gone to a so-called company-union basis after refusing to renew agreements with the stone-cutters' union, and members of the union in other states refused to handle the Bedford stone in

67

construction work. In upholding the injunction, the Supreme Court declared the union guilty of violating the Sherman Act.[1] Many other court decisions having a similar effect might be cited.

## DEPRESSION HARDSHIPS

When the depression came, after the 1929 stock-market crash, unemployment increased, and average hourly earnings in manufacturing had declined from 56 cents to 44 cents by 1933. But the Consumer Price Index declined even more sharply—from 51.3 in 1929 to 38.8 in 1933 (1967 = 100). By 1933, about 25 percent of the labor force were unemployed and others were on short work-weeks. Suffering was widespread, even though massive relief programs were devised by local, state, and national governments.

Corporate net profits declined from $8.6 billion in 1929 to minus $2.7 billion in 1932, obviously more than did money wages and much more than real wages. Net profits amounted to only $400 million in 1933, with losses suffered by an estimated 90 percent of all corporations. Indeed, not until 1941 did profits attain the 1929 level, even though the GNP and the size of the corporate sector of the economy had greatly enlarged. The working man was not the only victim of the depression.

Nevertheless, politicians and many intellectuals or liberals decided that drastic government action was needed to "correct the imbalance between the workers and the employers." In March 1931, Congress passed the Davis-Bacon Act, which required that employees of contractors performing federal-construction contracts in excess of $2,000 must be paid at least the wages "prevailing in the area in which the work was done."[2] In practice, this aided unions, as shown in Chapter XI.

In 1932, Congress passed and President Hoover signed the Norris-LaGuardia Act, drastically limiting the issuance of labor injunctions

---

1. Bedford versus Stone Cutters Association, 1927, 274 U. S. 37.

2. John P. Gould, *Davis-Bacon Act: The Economics of Prevailing Wage Laws* (Washington: American Enterprise Institute, 1971). The abuses and distortions in the administration of this law are explored.

by the federal courts. The stated purpose of the law was to build up the power of union officials and the unions.

In 1935 the Walsh-Healey law was enacted. This required that firms serving as parties to national-government contracts of $10,000 or more for materials, supplies, articles, or equipment must pay wages not less than the prevailing minimum wage in the locality, that wage to be ascertained by the secretary of labor. In practice, this often precluded nonunion firms from bidding on government contracts. Similar laws applied in many other situations where federal funds were involved. Many states adopted parallel laws. Three years later, in 1938, the Wage-and-Hour law, providing a nationwide minimum wage and penalties on overtime hours, was adopted.

In 1935 the Social Security law was enacted. Through numerous provisions, such as unemployment compensation, the law strengthened the determination of unions to hold out for higher settlements, even though in most states workers on strike were not directly eligible for benefits.

Regardless of the merit of some of this legislation, it did build up the power of union officials, while shifting the bargaining scales against the employer, with adverse impact on the consumer. It also prolonged the period of very high levels of unemployment until World War II was well under way.

Drawing upon the wording of the declaration of public policy in the Norris-LaGuardia Act, Section 7a of the National Industrial Recovery Act (NIRA), in 1933, stated that every restrictive industry code should provide that employees shall have the right to organize and bargain collectively through representatives of their own choosing, and shall be free from the interference, restraint, or coercion of employers of labor or their agents, or in the designation of such representatives, or in other activities carried on for the purpose of collective bargaining or of mutual aid or protection; no worker could be required, as a condition of employment, to join any company union, or to refrain from joining, organizing, or assisting a labor organization of his own choosing. . . .

The NIRA opened wide the door to unionism, while providing no safeguards against union abuses, and no protection whatever for employers. On May 27, 1935, the NIRA was declared unconstitutional by the Supreme Court; business practices were again subject to antitrust action. But the NIRA was replaced quickly (July 5, 1935) by the so-called Wagner Act—the National Labor Relations Act. It retained the one-sided features of the NIRA. This law, without precedent here or abroad, is possibly the most revolutionary law ever adopted in the United States. It was based on a complete misunderstanding of the nature of the labor market and of the market power of the employer. The subsequent wage-cost-push inflation can be largely attributed to this erroneous analysis.

The preamble of the Wagner Act asserts that the inequality of bargaining power between employers and employees who do not possess full freedom of association "tends to aggravate recurrent business depressions, by depressing wage rates and the purchasing power of wage-earners in industry and by preventing the stabilization of competitive wage rates and working conditions."

Here we have a new revelation! The purpose of the act is to "equalize bargaining power" and to take "wage rates and working conditions" out of competition. Put another way, the purpose is to create a labor monopoly.

According to the Wagner Act, the following were declared to be unfair employer practices (labeled unfair labor practices, however):

(1) to interfere with, restrain, or coerce employees in exercise of their rights of self-organization and collective bargaining,

(2) to encourage or discourage union membership by discrimination in regard to hire or tenure of employment or conditions of work, except such discrimination as may be involved in a closed shop agreement with a bona-fide union,

(3) to dominate or interfere with the formation or administration of any labor organization or contribute financial or other support to it,

(4) to refuse to bargain collectively with the representatives of his employees,

(5) to discharge or otherwise discriminate against an employee for filing charges or testifying under the Act.

A National Labor Relations Board (NLRB) was created to administer the law. Its record is one of bias against the employer (the consumer) and in favor of the union, the union official, and sometimes the union members. No unfair union practices were defined by the law. The board even reduced the employer's freedom of speech in a series of decisions as shown by Mary B. Peterson in *The Regulated Consumer.*

Congress allowed itself to confuse "inequality of bargaining power" with a slack labor market. In a depression, virtually all markets are slack—raw-material markets, finished-goods markets, capital-goods markets, financial and money markets, markets for rental property—there appear to be surpluses almost everywhere. The slack in the labor market is accompanied by reduced buying in all markets. Congress misread the evidence; hence its great mistakes.

Alchian and Allen, in their *University Economics,* effectively disposed of the very idea of labor's inferior bargaining power. After stating the usual arguments for the relative superiority of the bargaining power of the employer, they conclude, ". . . the fact is that the preceding argument is at best meaningless and at worst misleading or dead wrong." The employer pays what he must to recruit and keep a necessary labor force; the workers accept not their second-best offers, but their best offers. The authors point out that they have enormous bargaining power as individual professors in California, even though the state presumably has even greater bargaining power. Any time they feel like doing so, they can quit their jobs and take others that are slightly less rewarding; this, they say, is what forces California to pay them as well as it does. Bargaining power, they argue, derives from the rewards to be had in *other* jobs. But Congress did not understand all this, and does not to this day.

## SOME AMENDMENTS

The Taft-Hartley Act of 1947 (Labor Management Relations Act— LMRA) and the Landrum-Griffin Act of 1959 reduced somewhat the enormous powers that the depression-born legislation had granted to union officials, but not enough, as will be seen from the 1971 strike record described in the next chapter. And it had taken an unprecedented 5,000 strikes in 1946, involving 116 million man-days lost directly (plus others due to material delays, etc.) to make the passage of the first of these laws politically possible. In 1959, 3,700 strikes occurred, making the adoption of the second act possible. Work lost by nonstrikers in related or dependent enterprises and communities may exceed the work time lost by the strikers themselves. The Bureau of Labor Statistics makes no attempt to measure the full direct and indirect impact of man-days lost because of strikes.

That labor-management bargaining strength is still immensely one-sided is obvious. The world's most powerful companies are no match for the unions the law forces them to deal with. The 116-day strike of the steel-workers' union in 1959 against some 85 percent of our steel-making enterprises was settled only after the intervention of the vice president of the United States and other top government officials. Exactly eleven years later, in the autumn of 1970, the United Automobile Workers closed down the largest and most powerful manufacturing enterprise in the world (General Motors Corporation) for many weeks.

Closing down such a huge enterprise, along with many of its 30,000 suppliers, and damaging thousands of auto dealers did enormous harm. Workers lost pay; businessmen lost profits, many of them going into bankruptcy. The economic well-being of entire communities was seriously injured.

In 1964, during an earlier United Automobile Workers' strike against General Motors, *Time* magazine ran a news story under the heading "The Right Not To Work" (2 October 1964):

> The strike was as ill-timed and startling as a sneeze on a high wire—but, incredibly, there it was. Just when it seemed that the nation would be able to avoid trouble in the vital auto industry this year, and thus avoid possible upset to the advancing economy, Walter Reuther and the United Auto Workers hit the bricks against giant General Motors, whose daily operations affect the jobs and lives of countless Americans. And for what?

Showing the massive power of a single union official, the article went on:

In calling the strike, Reuther shrewdly did not pull out all of G.M.'s 345,000 U.A.W. workers, ordered plants that produce parts used by the other three automakers to continue working. By assuring the continued production of 1965 Ford, Chrysler and American Motors cars, he thus put added pressure on G.M. to settle.

How, one may ask, can Congress stand idly by, observing the exercise of this massive power—a power that Congress itself and its brainchild, the National Labor Relations Board, have turned over to union officials?

Referring to the legislation of the early 1930s, the Committee for Economic Development (CED) stated, "It is significant that these laws came at the depth of the Great Depression of the 1930s, when mass unemployment and great economic distress were widely interpreted as evidence that the workings of the market place could not adequately protect the interest of workers."[3] Even if the legislation had been good for the 1930s, it did not follow, the CED argued, that it was appropriate for periods of prosperity and inflationary conditions. Accordingly, the CED suggested a number of modest corrections, which the AFL-CIO quickly labeled "the same old union-busting witches' brew" *(Business Week,* 4 April 1964), and which Congress ignored. The imbalance persists. The consumer is victimized; inflation persists; and Congress does nothing to correct the egregious mistakes of earlier Congresses.

Usually business enterprises will not readily risk a strike. Inability to operate may quickly exhaust their working capital and credit. It may cause the permanent loss of markets and destroy the value of large sums the employers have invested in advertising and marketing. They may have much less staying power than the unions.

Milton Friedman and Anna Schwartz demonstrate quite conclusively that the severity and duration of the depression of the '30s were largely due to monetary and credit mistakes made by the FED. The money supply declined by more than a third from the peak of 1929 to the low of 1933. The FED literally wrung the money out of

3. *Union Powers and Union Functions: Toward a Better Balance* (New York: 964).

the economy; it extinguished more than one in every three dollars of money. This set powerful price deflation in motion and induced spending timidity and uncertainty.[4] Thus government, having made one massive mistake, proceeded to adopt a large number of prounion and labor-cost-raising laws from which our society has not yet recovered.

## CORRECTIVE DIAGNOSES

It is not clear that we have the intellectual and moral capacity to rid society of the debilitating laws, habits, and customs that grew out of the depression. Perhaps a crisis (like those of 1947, 1959, and 1971) may pave the way for reformation. But to achieve reform, opinion and thought leaders will need to understand the nature of past errors and of the necessary correctives. Only if we can develop a safe majority of informed opinion leaders can we take advantage of the opportunity the next crisis affords to reverse laws, customs, and habits, and adopt policies that are truly in the national interest.

There is no evidence at this writing that the plethora of strikes in 1946 and 1959, or those of 1971 when the economy appeared to be recovering from a mild recession, have awakened either the opinion-makers or the general public to the need for reducing and diffusing the powers that unions possess—powers so all-encompassing that the leaders must abuse them if they are to hold their positions.[5]

---

4. Milton Friedman and Anna Schwartz, *The Great Contraction—1929-33* (New York: National Bureau of Economic Research, 1963).

5. Lloyd Ulman, ed., *Challenges to Collective Bargaining* (Englewood Cliffs, N.J.: Prentice—Hall, Inc., 1967); some indecisive probing by labor economists occurs herein: A.H. Raskin, writer and an editor of *The New York Times* provides a hard-hitting realistic analysis of the labor problem. Why, he wonders, should union contracts have expiration dates?

# UNION POWER:
# THE 1971 RECORD

The year 1971, like 1946 and 1959, was marked by strikes and threats of strikes. The 1946 strikes persuaded Congress to pass the Taft-Hartley Act; those of 1959 produced the Landrum-Griffin Act; those of 1971 slowed down a hesitating economic recovery, helped greatly to defeat the administration's efforts to curb inflation and avoid a worsening of our international balance of payments, and persuaded a reluctant president to invoke wage-price controls utterly inconsistent with the philosophy of a free-market economy. Even more than the strikes of the earlier years, those of 1971 demonstrated the enormousness of the powers that union leaders had acquired.

It would be a serious error, of course, to conclude that excessive labor-union power was the sole cause of the international monetary crises of 1971 and the persistent rise in wage settlements and prices of that year. But the market power of labor unions substantially worsened the adverse developments.

## UNION POWER DEMONSTRATED IN 1971

In May, the Brotherhood of Railway Signalmen marked "Transportation Week" by shutting down the nation's railroads after the railroads thought they had established a pattern of sorts with the other railroad crafts when they accepted a government-board recommendation of a 42-percent wage increase spread over forty-two months. The signalmen, however, rejected this as "wholly inadequate" and insisted on a 54-percent increase, spread over thirty-six months. In the summer, the United Transportation Union, headed by Charles Luna, struck several railways at once, expecting to build up economic pressure on them.

In late July, a nationwide telephone strike ended when the Bell System agreed to raise pay 31 percent over a period of three years, with a first-year jump of 16 percent. The New York locals held out well into 1972 (with much violence and destruction of property).

At the last minute, in late July, the steel industry avoided a strike, against which it and its customers had stockpiled great quantities of steel, by granting a 31-percent increase plus an *unlimited ceiling* on cost-of-living adjustments—thereby helping to underwrite more cost escalation. *The Wall Street Journal,* on August 3, just twelve days before the president announced the wage-price freeze, prophetically editorialized:

> According to Steelworkers President I. W. Abel, the steel settlement was one of the most successful, if not the most successful, contract negotiations in the history of the Steelworkers. It's an open question just how many successes like this the union's members, the industry and the nation can stand.

In mid-1971 Harry Bridges' International Longshoremen's and Warehousemen's Union, called a strike that ran for 134 days, covering the Pacific Coast, including Hawaii and Alaska. Enormous damage was wreaked on farmers, shippers, importers, exporters, workers, investors, banks, and consumers.

On October 6, an eighty-day Taft-Hartley injunction suspended the strike until December 25, 1971. Negotiations having failed, the strike was resumed on January 17, 1972. Some exports and imports moved via Vancouver, B.C., and other Canadian ports, and Ensenada, Mexico. But the union took steps to shut off these sources of supplies and exports. Many markets were lost, some perhaps forever.

President Lyndon B. Johnson had promised to submit remedial legislation to Congress to stop such onslaughts, but he failed to act. President Nixon repeatedly urged the outlawing of these and similar strikes, but Congress failed to act—apparently figuring that the labor unions, with their concentrated and pinpointed political powers, had to be harkened to, while the widely dispersed shippers and consumers could be ignored.

On the East and the Gulf Coasts, the International Longshoremen's Association, headed by Thomas W. Gleason, went on strike on October 1, 1971. On November 26, an eighty-day Taft-Hartley injunction suspended the strike until February 14, 1972. The union president agreed to have the men work until March 14—hoping, presumably, to head off any new legislation and to wrest a more expensive contract from the shipowners. He said that his members were prepared to wait "until hell freezes over" to get their demands. Such tough talk and self-fulfilling prophecy in an emotional setting helps to create member solidarity and a serious fighting spirit. Bridges had argued that it requires lots of damage to win union demands.

After the wage-price freeze, Harry Bridges said, "We are telling Uncle Sam either he approves our settlement when we reach it or those lousy ships will stay tied up." How long? "Until all the damn money in the settlement is assured," he said. (*Business Week*, 4 September 1971.) Suppose ship or railway-company presidents had dared to talk that way to Uncle Sam? What a public clamor there would have been for severe penalties, and even the nationalization of the enterprises.

Our merchandise exports and imports combined amount to about $90 billion per annum, about 20 percent of which involved Canada and Mexico in 1971. Of the remainder, the operations of entire industries and often entire companies were virtually paralyzed by the strikes. Some imports came through a few docks not on strike; airline freight helped out, usually at great cost to shippers and consumers. And in anticipation of the strikes, some companies had stepped up importing and exporting.

The stoppage or substantial reduction of exports and imports in many communities, ports, industries, and enterprises had serious adverse impact on the less than strong economic-recovery forces in 1971 and early 1972. The unions involved caused much immediate and clearly measurable damage and hardship, as well as widespread

77

economic adversity all across the country, and extending to our trading partners in other countries.

The mayor of Honolulu, after fifty-five days of the strike on the West Coast, called for a socialized city-operated shipping line, after he declared a state of emergency. The governor advocated seizure of the Honolulu docks and the chartering of merchant ships.[1] The supply of numerous items essential for survival and to comfortable and sanitary living became scarce and even exhausted—toilet paper, for example.

On February 2, 1972, Harry Bridges, in testimony before a congressional committee, defied the United States government. He intimated that a world-wide tieup of U. S. ships might result if Congress intervened. He said, "We have a few friends in other countries and they will respond to our call for help . . . it may reach the point where the ships won't come back here." He threatened a slowdown of work and other devices to defy Congress, if he and his fellow officials could not get their way. In the U. S. Senate hearings, Bridges, when asked about the burden of the strike on the American people, responded, "My thinking is that winning this strike is the best thing for all workers." This is the tunnel vision all too typical of union officials.

The West-Coast strike ran 134 days, ending on February 19, 1972. Clearly, here is an example of market power, monopoly power, and even life-and-death power in the hands of union officials. The president of the United States, the secretary of labor, the chairman of the Federal Reserve System—and many other government officials at the national, state, and local levels—begged the union leaders to moderate their demands and bring the strikes to an end for the sake of humanity, forgetting that, as Simons warned long ago, "Monopoly power must be abused. It has no use save abuse." See page 3.

Thousands of enterprises adversely affected by strikes in their own plants, or among their suppliers or customers found themselves

---

1. For a revealing account of the damage and hardships see, "Labor: Dead Days on the Docks," *Time* magazine, 13 September 1971. Later, things got much worse; but the chairmen of the relevant Congressional committees and subcommittees remained virtually inert and immovable.

running out of working capital. Some were forced into bankruptcy; others had to borrow short-term funds to tide themselves over. Many deferred paying some of their bills. Others eliminated or cut their dividend rates, thereby slashing the incomes of thousands of stockholders, including foundations, mutual funds, and trusts. The asset values of security holdings declined. The Chesapeake and Ohio Railway, a strong well-managed enterprise, found its 1971 earnings cut to half of what they were the previous year, with a loss in the fourth quarter. The railroad was forced to omit its December quarter dividend. Strikes in rails, mines, and ports wreaked havoc.

Such episodes sent shock waves through the economy and retarded the weak recovery then under way. Thus it is not surprising that the general public is beginning to recognize the need to reduce and disperse undue private concentrations of power. Yet, and this *is* surprising, many of our elected representatives and appointed public officials seem disposed to curb strikes by seizing company assets (by what, in effect, amounts to nationalization of private enterprises) rather than union assets, although the struck companies would never have dared to close down whole industries as unions have done repeatedly.

Why union spokesmen favor "seizure of assets" (nationalization) is understandable, of course. As John S. Reed, president of the Santa Fe Railway, pointed out, they reason that if the railroads cannot meet their demands, the government can, and, on taking over, would have to. With tongue in cheek, he asked:

> Why not consider nationalizing the unions? Maybe they should have some federal management. It would cost next to nothing and would be immeasurably easier than nationalizing the railroads. If this sounds far-fetched, think about it a minute. The courts have already painted the unions as, in effect, quasi-governmental organizations enjoying by the leave of Congress an array of unique powers. Why not make them a little more quasi by attaching some meaningful responsibilities which would take into account the possible inflationary impact of demands, and which would make it possible for us to get genuine relief from makework rules and practices? I believe this could be done. (*Wall Street Journal,* 10 June 1971.)

## GOVERNMENT-EMPLOYEE UNIONS

Examining the strikes in 1971 by the municipal employees in New York City gives a hint of the enormous power of unions. One of the most dramatic of the public-be-damned strike actions took place in June, when the Municipal Employees Union left twenty-seven of the city's twenty-nine movable bridges—many of them stripped by employees of critical parts—inaccessible to motorists. Buses, trucks, and hundreds of thousands of motorists were trapped in huge traffic jams on the hottest day of the year.[2] Engines overheated and failed to operate. Working people, including executive and professional personnel, were unable to keep commitments. The strikers had stolen essential parts of the bridges and keys to lock and unlock parts for opening and closing them, and had damaged crucial parts and components. The Army Corps of Engineers dispatched crews to act in "an advisory capacity only" to municipal administrative personnel! Victor H. Gotbaum, head of the striking union, won approval to enlarge the onslaught on New Yorkers, and defiantly said that he was willing to go to jail.

Mayor John V. Lindsay, though usually friendly to unions, did call the strike of the city workers "immoral, illegal, outrageous and offensive to the public interest." But the union stepped up its guerrilla warfare by closing down most of the city's sewage-treatment plants, which had been processing 1.3 billion gallons of raw sewage daily. The strikers allowed raw, untreated sewage to flow directly into the East and Hudson Rivers. Firemen at city incinerators, park-department foremen and gardeners, water-supply and board-of-education employees also abandoned their jobs. In the ninety-degree heat, youngsters opened fire hydrants, lowering the water pressure to danger points in many cases.

*The New York Times,* on June 8, editorialized:

> The outrageous strike by unionized municipal employees that made a shambles of traffic yesterday, endangered lives, jeopardized the water supply and threw a spreading paralysis over other city services demonstrates how completely New York City has become prisoner of its pampered civil service unions.

2. See *The New York Times,* 8 June 1971 for stories and photos.

IN JUNE 1971 THE NEW YORK CITY BRIDGE TENDERS' STRIKE LEFT 27 OF THE CITY'S 29 MOVABLE BRIDGES INACCESSIBLE TO MOTORISTS. HUNDREDS OF THOUSANDS OF VEHICLES WERE TRAPPED IN TRAFFIC JAMS ON THE HOTTEST DAY OF THE YEAR.

Referring to the union head, the *Times* said:

> If he and his followers continue to put themselves above
> considerations of law and public safety, it is incumbent on
> Mayor and Governor to forget their feud, restore use of
> the bridges through police or National Guard, and unite in
> whatever other measures are necessary to restore full city
> services. Arguments over the tax package are secondary to
> an emphatic assertion of the city's right to function free of
> blackjacking by its civil service unions or anyone else.

New York City has suffered through and been permanently damaged by numerous other strikes. The city, some observers have said,
is now ungovernable. I. D. Robbins, a close student of municipal
affairs and finances, and a trustee and past president of the City Club
of New York, sized up the fiscal plight of the city:

> The municipal unions have demonstrated their ability to
> cause city officials to meet any demands they have the
> nerve to ask for. It is unlikely that city officials, who by
> and large depend on municipal unions and their families as
> part of their political combination, will act to avoid union
> exactions. Hard-pressed cities will have to hope for some
> stiffening by governors and legislators. Legislatures could
> be asked to change or suspend certain unproductive fringe
> benefits or to restrict the bargaining right of cities or at
> least to require that all union agreements be ratified by the
> local legislative body so that responsibility is fixed.
>
> It may be said that all of these ideas are unacceptable to
> politicians and, therefore, probably can't be adopted. But
> to reject them is to say that there is almost nothing the
> cities can do for themselves.

The Brookings Institution, in announcing a new publication,
stated:

> The emergence of militant unionism among municipal em-
> ployees has spawned numerous issues that require quick
> and careful attention. The authors of this first book in the
> Brookings series of Studies of Unionism in Government
> define the issues and suggest ways of coping with them.
> Specifically, they are concerned with the applicability of
> collective bargaining to the public sector and challenge the

proposition that what is good for public employees is good for the cities, counties, and states.[3]

Collective bargaining in the public sector of our society calls for a new name. The union officials and members, in effect, sit on both sides of the bargaining table. In many cases they "control city hall," or at least the balance of power in local government, and, of course, they instigate union demands and have massive power to see that they are met. Politicians rely on union support when they run for office, and they make payment in full when the union officials come hat-in-hand demanding more money, shorter hours, more paid holidays, and more fringe benefits. Furthermore, the relationship impairs on-the-job discipline, productivity, and work effort.[4]

The competitive pressures operating in the private sector are completely absent in the public. The major daily newspapers in Washington, D.C., each have one or more columnists writing on labor and unions in government. They often cite remarkable examples of tardiness, absenteeism, loafing, politicking, and scheming against their agency or division heads and against the taxpayer. So far no researcher has mined the rich ores embedded in these newspaper columns.

On the general problem, Kurt L. Hanslowe of Cornell University, former assistant counsel of the UAW, said:

> The union shop in public employment has the potential of becoming a neat mutual back-scratching mechanism, whereby public employee representatives and politicians each reinforce the others' interest and domain, with the public employee and the individual citizen left to look on, while his employment conditions, his tax rate and public policies generally are decided by entrenched and mutually supportive government officials and collective bargaining representatives over whom the public has diminishing control.[5]

---

3. Harry H. Wellington and Ralph K. Winter, *The Unions and the Cities* (Washington: The Brookings Institution, 1971).

4. Daniel H. Kruger, et al. *Collective Bargaining in the Public Service* (New York: Random House, 1969).

5. Shirley Scheibla, "Public Servant—or Master?" *Barron's Weekly*, New York, 17 April 1972, p. 9.

The same story could be told of 1971 strikes, or threats of strikes, by school teachers, by city transportation employees, and by workers in aluminum, copper, metal can, and other industries. When the wage-price freeze was announced by President Nixon in mid-August, some 350 strikes were in progress, and others threatened.

In the fall of 1971 the United Mine Workers union, covering most of our coal mining, went on a strike that continued for more than a month, widely impairing fuel supplies. This skewed railroad operations by reducing cargo, and deprived many people in the mining communities. The Pay Board granted the union wage-fringe increases in excess of 16 percent for the first year, even though the board's own target ceiling was 5.5 percent. It broke its ceiling only because the miners simply would otherwise have refused to work, government ruling or no.

Backing down before such defiance only encourages more of it. Too many labor unions already operate virtually as sovereign governments, above the law, and free from the restraints that apply to all other private associations and organizations. How long will such virtual anarchy be tolerated? The answer is: as long as giant unions controlling entire industries are allowed to retain their present monopolistic powers. Great cities and even the largest companies remain at their mercy.

"Free" collective bargaining, to quote *The Economist* (London, 24 September 1966) is seen by more and more people as "collective clobbering." Lamenting the confused popular thinking, *The Economist*, noting that the United Kingdom had taken steps to restrain monopoly in the goods markets, said, "There are no equivalent weapons in being against the monopoly activities of trade unions. . . . That this activity must now be brought under at least some statutory restraint is obvious." Even though the United Kingdom did adopt some strong industrial relations legislation in 1971, the country suffered a six-week coal strike, the most damaging strike in its history, in early 1972. In numerous subsequent strikes, union officials not only ignored the law and court orders, but defiantly asserted that they would not abide by them.

Clearly, the late Roscoe Pound, dean of Harvard Law School, was correct when he assigned the blame for the current situation to the special immunities, exemptions, and privileges that were granted to unions and their officials and denied to all other private groups and their representatives:

> ... to commit wrongs to persons and property, to inter-fere with the use of highways, to break contracts, to deprive individual workers and their local organizations by national organizations centrally and arbitrarily adminis-tered beyond the reach of state laws, and to misuse trust funds—things which no one else can do with impunity.[6]

The Landrum-Griffin Act of 1959 checked some labor abuses, but the strikes discussed in this chapter betrayed the inadequacy of the restraints so far imposed. Increasingly, thoughtful people are asking themselves whether anything short of outlawing collective bargain-ing—something all totalitarian governments do as a matter of course—can bring relief. Such drastic action is avoidable only if we are prepared to rescind the special immunities and privileges extended to unions.

Collective bargaining has come to have many of the characteristics of armed robbery, and to look like another manifestation of the breakdown of law and order.

## UNIONS' SOURCE OF ECONOMIC UNCERTAINTY

The major strikes and strike threats in late 1970, and extending into 1971, disrupted the economy and created costly uncertainties that impaired business planning and forced economists to condition every business-appraisal outlook on the outcome of strike threats and actual strikes.

The UAW strike against General Motors in the fall of 1970 led to a build-up of motor-vehicle inventories. During the two-month strike, the entire economy, already in a mild recession, was pulled down further. After the strike was settled, late in 1970, the subsequent restocking gave the economy a short-run boost. But neither business-

---

6. Roscoe Pound, *Legal Immunities of Labor Unions* (Washington: American Enterprise Institute, 1958).

men nor economists could determine whether the recovery was durable, or merely a catch-up spurt, or how much of each.

Similarly, the threat of a steel strike in early 1971 caused producers and users of steel to build up inventories. Again, business and economic observers found it difficult to disentangle the economic activity that was "normal recovery" from the part that was strike-threat induced. In the summer, no steel strike occurred, but the damage was done to employees in steel and elsewhere, to businessmen and owners and to their creditors, suppliers, and customers. The chart below shows the shift in steel output during the year. Clearly this must have been disruptive of the affairs and lives of countless workers and their families and of enterprises and activities dependent upon continuity.

CHART 7

STEEL PRODUCTION

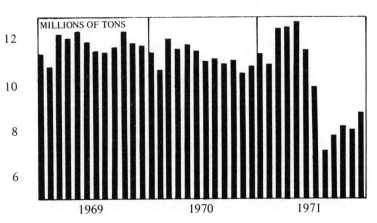

Before and during steel strikes (or strike threats), steel imports mount. If our own steel sources are unreliable, steel users will take steps to protect themselves. After each such episode, steel imports constitute a higher proportion of our steel consumption than before.[7] Then pressures build up for import quotas or higher tariffs on steel. More than a hundred-million consumers pay and pay.

The nationwide coal-miners' strike in the fall of 1971 upset the calculations of countless observers, including the government officials responsible for economic-policy implementation. The enormous disruptions of the dock strikes on the East, the Gulf, and the West Coasts including Hawaii, adversely affected every major retailer in the country—as well as countless small enterprises dependent on imports of raw material, parts and components, or finished goods. The damage ran into the hundreds of millions of dollars.

Uncertainty is costly. It finds its way into the prices of everything consumers buy. That it is invisible to most people does not negate its adverse impact. Economists and businessmen and their bankers and advisers spend much time and effort appraising the business and economic outlook. Millions of buying and selling decisions are heavily conditioned by their assessments. The trade press and the economic divisions of most news media devote much space to these uncertainties. Quarterly and annual reports of individual corporations show similar concern.

The labor union is thus a powerful producer of uncertainty and, therefore, a costly institution. Whether unionized employees should be allowed to continue to create such havoc is a question we will face with increasing concern as government assumes more and more responsibility for full employment and we all become more and more interdependent.

---

7. Senate Finance Committee, Staff Report, R. M. Weidenhammer, Co-ordinator, *Steel Imports* (Washington: Government Printing Office, December 1967).

# MONETARY AND FISCAL POLICIES VERSUS THE WAGE PUSH

Can inflation be controlled by monetary and fiscal policies, or must they be supplemented by policies that will effectively trim the power of union officials? Competent objective economists are divided on this question.

All agree that inflation is primarily a monetary problem. Friedman, the leader of the so-called monetarist school of economic analysis, insists that, "Inflation is always and everywhere a monetary phenomen." He has said that he knew of no instance in history where inflation was not preceded by a substantial expansion in the money stock in excess of production, and no case where the money stock was brought under control that was not followed by an abatement of inflation. Few scholars would disagree. Friedman took a strong position against the "incomes policy" adopted in 1971.[1]

Haberler, on the other hand, while agreeing that inflation is basically a momentary phenomenon, is convinced that union power must be reduced. Otherwise, he believes, all the other measures suggested for fighting inflation would be in vain. He insists that wage-push is a reality that urgently calls for remedial action.[2]

After 1968, with rising inflation, rising unemployment, and withal, rising wage rates, a number of economists who were formerly in the Friedman camp changed positions, concluding with Haberler

---

1. Friedman, *Newsweek,* 28 September 1970.
2. Gottfried Haberler, *Incomes Policies and Inflation—An Analysis of Basic Principles* (Washington: American Enterprise Institute, 1971).

that wage-push called for some strong supplementary policies. But stress on some form of "incomes policy" or labor-union reform predates recent years. The rise in wages during the economic slack in the late 1950s produced a considerable spate of scholarly works, a few of which we note here.

## WAGE-PUSH IN THE 1950s

*The Economic Analysis of Labor Union Power,* first published in 1958, and revised in 1963, is the work of the late Dr. Edward H. Chamberlin of Harvard University. Chamberlin had long been recognized as one of the world's leading authorities on competition and monopoly. In an address in Washington, D.C., (January 16, 1959), he noted that the concentration of economic power in the labor field was very great and could operate with virtually no restriction, in part because so few people are aware of it at all. He went on to say:

> Nobody is surprised if higher raw-material costs increase the price of the finished product; so why it should be thought that higher labor costs would have the special property of coming out of profits without affecting prices is a major mystery. In other words, the gains of any particular concentration of labor power are paid in the end by the general consuming public, as surely as are those of industrial monopoly. The public has exactly as much interest in the terms of the contract between labor and management, as it has in industrial prices and in the prices of commodities at retail which it purchases directly. And the fact that it doesn't know it is one of the major sources of power in the hands of the labor union. . . .[3]

Chamberlin stressed the fact that under collective bargaining the power of the union materially affects costs, and one of the oldest and most respected economic laws states that the price of a commodity tends to equal its costs. Thus, in the report mentioned above he stated:

---

3. Dr. Edward H. Chamberlin, *The Economic Analysis of Labor Union Power* (Washington: American Enterprise Institute, 1963 ed.).

90

It is fundamental to distinguish between the labor market and the product market, but it is also common to place far too much emphasis on the distinction. As markets, they are clearly not the same: the former deals with the purchase and sale of labor services, the latter with the purchase and sale of the company's product. The link between them, however, is simple and vital—that the buyer in the first market and the seller in the second are one and the same, viz the entrepreneur. Another way to state the relationship is that the entrepreneur buys labor in the first market for the obvious purpose of reselling it, incorporated into a product, in the second. The economic law which links the two markets, the "law of cost," is as venerable and respectable among economists as the more famous "law of supply and demand." In simplest form it states that the price of a commodity tends to equal its cost of production. . . .[4]

Of course, union officials in their sales-promotion literature and speeches, continuously take credit, frequently all of it, for raising wages. If they merit this credit, can they shrug off price effects in the product market? Professor Walter A. Morton of the University of Wisconsin put the matter this way; "The purpose, aim, function and objective of labor unions is to exert a wage-push,"[5] a push, let it be noted, that is primarily against consumer, rather than owner interests. This, of course, only means that we should examine objectively not only the stated union purposes or goals, but also, and more important, their strength and how they, along with other forces, operate with what results on the market. Care must be taken, too, not to confuse all wage increases with an inflationary wage-push.

Chamberlin continued his analysis with these observations:

So it is that a modern theory of wages, which recognizes the power in the hands of groups of laborers by direct action to raise their money incomes permits recognition of

---

4. Ibid. Heavy reliance on Chamberlin and other publications of the American Enterprise Institute is with the permission of the publisher. The same is the case of reliance on *Inflation, Unions and Wage Policy*, Washington: Chamber of Commerce of the United States, 1960, as well as its other publications.

5. Walter A. Morton, *Annual Proceedings*, Industrial Relations Research Association, December 1958.

the possible role played by organized labor in the inflationary process. "Wage-push inflation" is logically inconsistent with a purely *competitive*[6] labor market, and it will naturally be denied by many, among whom will be those whose thinking continues to run in "competitive" terms. Such an account of inflation is "new" in the sense that it runs counter to the traditional view in which prices are *pulled* up by demand (either by monetary expansion or by increase in "spending"), rather than *pushed* up by costs. But both are possible and *neither excludes the other.*

There seems to be no reason to doubt that the upward pressures exerted by unions and transmitted to prices through the law of costs may well proceed (as they have recently) at a rate greater than the rate of increase in productivity for the economy as a whole, with a resulting general rise in prices. . . .

Chamberlin's approach is not an either-or analysis in terms of the cost-push versus monetary explanation of inflation. He recognizes the role of each and does not accept the view that one must embrace one or the other.[7] Nor can we ignore the misallocation of resources and the economic distortions that follow differential union settlements.

He also points out the fallacy of the claims that wage increases are paid out of profits without price effects—and are, therefore, noninflationary. Thus, Chamberlin further stated:

The notion is common that a wage increase impinges mainly on profits and hence need have no effect on prices at all. Of course this may happen in certain cases and to a

---

6. The important thing to remember in this connection is that the labor market has been rendered noncompetitive for the given employer as a buyer.

7. Many other authors, who place credence in the wage-push explanation of inflation might be cited. The late Professor Sumner H. Slichter is perhaps the most widely known exponent of this view, although he, like most others, regarded it as only one of the factors. Most of the more than two dozen contributors to two volumes either explicitly or implicitly follow this pattern: Philip Bradley, ed., *The Public Stake in Union Power* (Charlottesville: University of Virginia Press, 1959); Charles A. Myers, ed., *Wages, Prices, Profits and Productivity* (New York: Columbia University Press, 1959).

limited extent, but such an effect is typically only a short-run phenomenon, and the run may be very short indeed. Profits are no more available than are other cost outlays as a source from which increased labor income may be met without affecting prices.

It should be noted that the frequent claim by labor that profits are "adequate" to afford a wage increase without raising prices contains within itself the seeds of a vicious price spiral. It may be a factor in winning an actual wage increase, perhaps by gaining a measure of public support in one form or another for the labor side. But since labor cannot deny to the employer his natural defensive move of a price adjustment if market conditions make it possible, the original condition of profits supposedly "adequate" for a wage increase is likely soon to be restored, and the cycle begins again. The flaw in the argument is to suppose that the businessman (or labor or anyone else) will not normally conduct his affairs with full reference to the advantages (and limitations) which are set for him by the competitive situation in which he finds himself. . . .

The idea that price or profit restraint will induce wage-demand restraint keeps cropping up; yet, there is little evidence of the general validity of the idea. Friedman, although dubious about wage-push as a cause of inflation, would not disagree with this analysis; thus he noted how the heavy union demands during the feeble recovery period 1933-37 contributed strongly to the 1937 relapse.[8]

On occasion, union officials may tailor their demands to an industry situation. But rarely. In 1958, for instance, when a recession was on, union officials in Britain demanded and got inflationary wage increases—with one of their claims being that these would cure the recession. *The Economist* reviewing the third report of the Cohen Council (established in Great Britain to deal with the wage-price spiral and full-employment complex), stated:

It is a tempting idea to the Left that discriminatory government action against dividends or profits might induce union leaders themselves to go slow on wage claims,

---

8. Friedman *Guidelines, Informal Controls and the Market Place,* edited by George P. Shultz and R. Z. Aliber (Chicago: University of Chicago Press, 1966).

even while a climate of public opinion remains that would in the end allow most of those claims to be granted; but the idea is moonshine. Some of the most publicised wage battles during recent years of both boom and recession have been against nationalised industries which, so far from making exorbitant profits, have been making large losses. . . .[9]

The most damaging strike in the United Kingdom since the general strike of 1926 occurred in 1972, when the coal miners quit at a time when the socialized coal industry was taking large losses. In June 1972, the United Kingdom authorities let the pound float, after failures to restrain wage increases. Government employee unions, in New York City as we have seen, showed an identical lack of restraint, even though the city is on the verge of insolvency.

There is a great contrast between bargaining as the term is used in labor-management relations and as it is used in ordinary conversation or general economic literature. Chamberlin suggests that we might enlighten ourselves if we apply the labor union bargaining techniques to some other market and see what happens. Chamberlin uses the sale of a house to bring the point home:

If A is bargaining with B over the sale of A's house, and if A were given the privileges of a modern labor union, he would be able (1) to conspire with all other owners of houses not to make any alternative offer to B, using violence or the threat of violence if necessary to prevent them, (2) to deprive B himself of access to any alternative offers, (3) to surround the house of B and cut off all deliveries, including food (except by parcel post[10]), (4) to stop all movement from B's house, so that if he were for instance a doctor he could not sell his services and make a living, and (5) to institute a boycott of B's business. All of these privileges, if he were capable of carrying them out, would no doubt strengthen A's position. But they would not be regarded by anyone as a part of bargaining—unless A were a labor union.

---

9. *The Economist,* 15 August 1959, p. 396.
10. An actual case in Massachusetts.

Why do lenders or borrowers not engage in similar tactics? Why do not buyers of timber, lumber, or furniture bludgeon the sellers, and bring coercive measures to bear so as to get a fair deal? Why do our automobile companies, tire manufacturers, or appliance producers rely on free volunatry consumer choice to make their sales?

What would happen if all of these buyers and sellers relied on boycotts, picketing, violence; and coercion to make a sale and dispose of their products? What would the activist professors, the politicians, reporters and editors, and the union officials do and say? What would you and I, as consumers, or voters, say and do? Yet union officials, and often the members, regard having the power to act in this way as evidence of public virtue; then aggressiveness is encouraged.

In 1958, the same year in which Chamberlin's *The Economic Analysis of the Labor Union Power* first appeared, Dr. Harold G. Moulton, former president of the Brookings Institution, came quite independently to much the same conclusion in his *Can Inflation Be Controlled?*:

> It is impossible . . . to escape the conclusion that the factor primarily responsible for the progressive advance in prices in recent decades has been the extraordinary rise in wage rates—the major element in costs of production. The fact that prices did not rise in proportion to the advance in wage costs is attributable chiefly to improvements in operating efficiency. . . .[11]

Moulton concluded:

> On the cost side, it appears certain that continuing increases in wage rates will be a powerful force working for progressively higher prices of industrial products. The wage item (embedded in raw materials, transportation, fuel and power, as well as directly in the manufacturing process) has, as we have seen, become of preponderant importance. And the economic and political power of modern labor

---

11. Harold G. Moulton, *Can Inflation Be Controlled?* (Washington, D.C.: Anderson Kramer Associates, 1958), p. 163. For a sympathetic review of Moulton's book, see *American Economic Review*, June 1959, p. 453; for another review, see *The Economist*, 7 February 1959.

organizations is such that continued pressure for higher rates of pay is to be expected. Escalator clauses in labor contracts, designed to lessen industrial strife, serve to accelerate the inflation process. . . . [12]

Housewives, he might have said, don't run around from store to store bidding up or pulling up prices. "Demand-pull" is the wrong phrase. Moulton marshals considerable evidence against the "demand-pull" theory of inflation. He argues that prices are set, for the most part, on the basis of costs ascertained and established *before* goods come onto the market where demand forces could play their roles. His examination of the differential behavior of wholesale and retail prices led him to conclude that pressures come first on wholesale, basic, raw materials and are transmitted by costs, not by demand. Rising costs are the forces, he argues, that most generally establish higher prices. Friedman used closely similar language in his column in *Newsweek* of September 28, 1970, but drew an opposite conclusion.

After examining the various explanations of how, in the private economy, additional money gets into circulation and how the prices changing process works, Moulton said:

> An increase in the supply of gold or an expansion of bank credit can increase the flow of money income to the people only if there is occurring an increase in rents, wages, interest, and profits. Since there are no other circuits than these pay envelopes there can be no independent "inflating" or blowing up of the money supply; no automatic "pumping" or "injecting" money into the channels of circulation. It follows that the aggregate money income available for expenditure can be expanded, appreciably, only by an increased flow through pay envelopes.
>
> Thus we arrive at the conclusion: The supply of money as compared with the supply of goods is governed by the ratio of rates of pay to productive output. Accordingly, if we are to understand the price-changing process we must analyze the forces operating within the productive system to increase or decrease rates of pay as compared with output. . . . [13]

12. Ibid., p. 171. For a discussion of the impact of wage escalation clauses on inflation, see article in *Nation's Business,* September 1959.

13. Ibid., pp. 47-48.

In *Forecasting the Price Level,* Sidney Weintraub of the University of Pennsylvania came to conclusions similar to Moulton's. Weintraub categorically concludes, "The wage level, not the money supply, governs the price level. . . ."[14] Thus Chamberlin, Moulton, and Weintraub, employing similar approaches, reinforce one another.

Even earlier, Schumpeter who was not only a most careful student of money, credit, and inflation, but had lived through several major inflations, had this to say:

> Now it is evidently possible to say . . . that the whole trouble is "increase in the quantity of money." But since this increase in the quantity of money is an incident in a process that involves more fundamentally "causal elements" . . . it is equally possible to say that the bank or banks which finance the increase in both government and business expenditure are playing a "passive" role and . . . are but "responding to the needs" that have arisen in consequence of high prices and high money wages. . . . Neither of these two statements is necessarily erroneous. But each of them becomes erroneous as soon as it is interpreted to deny the element that the other one emphasizes. . . .[15]

## REVIVAL OF WAGE-PUSH CONCERN IN THE 1970s

Dr. Arthur F. Burns, chairman of the Federal Reserve System, was somewhat surprised, in 1970, that monetary and fiscal policies seemed ineffectual in restraining undue wage increases in slack times, and in stopping inflation. In testimony before the Joint Economic Committee (July 23, 1971, just three weeks before the Nixon wage-price freeze), Dr. Burns presented the familiar data showing that unemployment and prices were not responding to monetary and fiscal policies as expected. He said, "Strong and stubborn inflationary forces, emanating from rising costs, linger on. . . . I cannot help but wonder . . . whether our recent experience with wage settlements in unionized industries may not reflect a gradual shift in the

---

14. Sidney Weintraub, *Forecasting the Price Level, Income Distribution and Economic Growth* (New York: Chilton Co., 1959).

15. Schumpeter, *Nation's Business,* June 1948.

balance of power at the bargaining table." By "recent" he appeared to refer to the previous year or two. Actually, as we have seen, the imbalance was of much earlier vintage, but, for various reasons, it had recently become more pernicious.

Dr. Burns was among the earliest of top government officials to stress the existence of wage-push inflation and the need for some form of "incomes policies" that would improve the workings of the labor market. In a speech on December 7, 1970, he asserted that government efforts to achieve price stability were being thwarted by wage increases in excess of productivity gains. He said, "The inflation that we are still experiencing is no longer due to excess demand. It rests rather on the upward push of costs—mainly, sharply rising wage rates."

Dr. Burns urged that we take steps to make the market operate with greatly reduced impediments rather than via rigid controls. He suggested an increase in our oil and other commodity import quotas and more vigorous enforcement of the antitrust laws. But his primary stress was on improved labor markets. To this end, he urged better job-training programs, the creation of productivity councils on a nationwide basis, a more aggressive program of establishing computerized job banks, suspension of the Davis-Bacon Act—which pushed up federal construction costs—modification of the minimum-wage law to improve job opportunities for teenagers, the establishment of national building codes, compulsory arbitration of labor disputes in certain industries, and improved depreciation policies to encourage faster write-off of old and obsolescent equipment. He thought it might be desirable to set up a voluntary high-level price-and-wage review board, with authority to investigate, advise, and *recommend* price and wage changes. He did not advise economy-wide wage and price controls.

Seven months later, in his July 23 testimony for some form of "incomes policy," Burns said, "In my judgment, and in the judgment of the Board as a whole, the present inflation in the midst of substantial unemployment poses a problem that traditional monetary and fiscal remedies cannot solve as quickly as the national interest demands." Three weeks later, President Nixon announced the wage-price freeze (August 15, 1971).

98

Dr. Gardner Ackley of the University of Michigan, chairman of the President's Council of Economic Advisers during most of President Johnson's tenure, employed strong language in condemnation of excessive union power:

> It seems crystal clear to me that an incomes policy is meaningless unless—among other things—it aims directly at reducing the excessive wage gains made by the powerful unions. I don't mean the lettuce pickers, the hospital workers, or even the textile workers. I mean instead unions like the United Automobile Workers, the Teamsters, and the Steel Workers. These are groups whose members are not exactly poor. For example, something like 75 percent of American families—including those with more than one wage earner—receive annual incomes lower than the average auto worker earns.

Ackley noted that under the General 'Motors Corporation-UAW contract signed after a long UAW strike in the autumn of 1970:

> We are told that the *average* annual earnings of auto workers in 1973 will fall between $12,000 and $13,000, in addition to some of the most complete and expensive fringe benefits found anywhere—such as retirement with a $6,000 pension at age 56. There are many highly respected four-year colleges in which the *average* wage of the faculty—excluding janitors, secretaries, clerks, etc.—is no higher than $12,000.[16]

Here Dr. Ackley clearly implied that sectional collective bargaining had failed to yield justice or equity; nonetheless he failed to take any position with respect to the retention of collective bargaining, despite the frankness of his denunciation of·its exercise by the big unions.

Edwin L. Dale, a columnist and editorial writer for *The New York Times,* advanced a potent argument against those who, with "ritual neutralism" (to use a Dr. George Terborgh animadversion) automatically, by force of habit or otherwise, ascribe cost-push inflation

---

16. Address 18th Annual Conference on the Economic Outlook, University of Michigan, 19 November 1970.

to "economic or market power," *both* in the goods market *and* in the labor market. "Public debate and discussion," Dale said, "of the present inflation [January, 1971] issue has been bedeviled by a fatal semantic error: the use of the term 'wage and price problem.' It is a wage problem and it will not be solved until the 'plague-on-both-your-houses' mentality is overcome. Corporate profits, no matter how measured, are not the culprit now." (*New York Times Magazine,* January 3, 1971.) *Look* magazine was sufficiently impressed by Dale's candor and logic to republish the article in full on February 23, 1971.

Despite Dale's telling analysis, politicians and key government officials continued to repeat the "wage-price spiral" phrase as though nothing had been said. Ritual neutralists live and speak, oblivious of the rapid rise of wage-fringe increases and the slower rise of prices and thinning of profit margins. And the wage-price freeze continued this neutralism, possibly a politically inevitable combination. Even Burns, in his testimony before the Joint Economic Committee on February 9, 1972, retreated into this same formulation, with no discrimination as to the source of sustained upward cost pressures.

Haberler believes that some form of controls or "incomes policy" has become the most urgent problem of macroeconomic policy in almost all industrial countries. The growth of unionism, increased union militancy, and the unionization of white-collar workers and government employees have made wage-push inflation in many countries a serious or even menacing problem, he says, "jeopardizing stability, growth, and employment."

It is often said that because only 23 percent of the labor force is unionized, unions cannot be all that powerful. Actually, eliminating the self-employed and the small outfits with one- or two-dozen employees, not much under one-third of the work force is now unionized. Furthermore, in contrast to the situation of several decades ago, unionism now has permeated all sectors of the economy. Prior to World War II, only a few major sectors were heavily unionized: large-scale construction, printing, transportation, mining, and parts of manufacturing. Today local unions, usually affiliated with national and international units, are found in all cities, all towns, and even many villages and rural areas in which substantial employment centers are located. Employees of most manufacturing firms are unionized. Unionism is in the air, it is widespread. Its propaganda, its sales literature, its spokesmen are everywhere. Union activities, including strike and demand pronouncements are front-page copy. The unionization of teachers and other public employees has made politicians much more fearful of union onslaughts. White-collar workers are well represented among the union members. News-media employees and entertainers, actors and actresses are unionized.

All this creates quite a different problem for the firm not yet unionized, as well as for the consumer and the public. Confronted with unionism on every side, the employer must react to the changes in working conditions, wages, and fringes in the union sectors, if he is to avoid unionization of his own firm. The spillover effect of union-ism today greatly exceeds that of the prewar era. All this makes wage-push much more potent, much more likely. Union officials, too, are more aware of the scope of their powers and are, therefore, more aggressive and bolder.

Haberler recognizes the monetary element in both demand-pull and wage-push inflation. Monetary restraint may reduce demand-pull inflation with only a slight and temporary adverse effect on output and employment. But counteracting a cost-push inflation with mone-tary restraint will create some lasting unemployment and a corres-ponding loss of output. Haberler states:

> Thus the existence of powerful trade unions—labor monopolies—which force up money wages by strikes, or the threat of strikes confronts the monetary authorities with a disagreeable dilemma: Either they can create enough money to permit the rise in prices that is com-patible with the rise in wages, or they can prevent inflation by refusing to expand monetary circulation, but only at the cost of "creating" a sufficient amount of unemploy-ment to stop the wage-push.

Unions, with rare exceptions, insist on *annual* wage increases (or more often, under CPI-escalator clauses). Such trends spread through much of the rest of the economy.

Politicians regard it as mandatory to take a strong position against unemployment. Even when the target rate for tolerable unemployment was 4 percent, in the early 1960s, a rise of only one or two percentage points to 5 or 6 percent was pronounced "totally intolerable," etc.

Dr. William Fellner of Yale concluded that even without a wage-push from the unions, ". . . there seems to be little controversy about the distinctly inflationary implications of the four percent unemployment target. . . ." and a higher rate is politically unacceptable. With unions in the picture, the rate of inflation will tend to accelerate. Fellner's analysis assumes a permissive monetary-fiscal policy.[17] For a more complete analysis of the wage-push realities, a careful study of Haberler's report is rewarding.

## ECONOMISTS FROM ABROAD

Professor James E. Meade of Cambridge University has reluctantly concluded that unions do cause a wage-push that must somehow be thwarted, though we must rely primarily on monetary and fiscal policies. To mitigate the wage-push, Meade suggested that the government set a "norm" for permissible annual wage increases. Any group of employers and employees could, if both agreed, exceed this norm. In case of dispute, a tribunal or court set up for the purpose would determine whether a particular wage claim would cause the earnings of the workers to exceed the previous earnings by more than the norm. If so, then certain controls would operate. Any workers who went on strike in favor of the claim would lose any accumulated rights to redundancy payments in their existing jobs, and any supplementary benefits paid for the support of their families would become a liability of the trade union supporting the strike, or, failing that, would be treated as a debt of the individual worker concerned. Further, the trade union would be liable to a tax on any strike benefits paid to its members. But there would be no curb on union bargaining in regard to claims that did not exceed the government norm.

17. William Fellner, *Aiming for a Sustainable Second Best During the Recovery from the 1970 Recession* (Washington: American Enterprise Institute, 1971). Dr. George Terborgh in his *Essays on Inflation* had come to the same conclusions (Washington: Machinery and Allied Products Institute, 1971).

These were tentative suggestions, subject to refinement and improvement. Meade did not hesitate to conclude:

> I think we must squarely face the fact that trade unions *are* monopolistic organizations in which individuals have banded together to fix a price for what they are selling and that with the present rules and regulations these particular monopolistic bodies have too great a bargaining power. . . . Indeed, in no other sphere of economic life does one consider it desirable that a monopolistic organization should not be subject to social controls of one kind or another over such matters as the prices it charges or the amount it supplies.[18]

In a foreword to Meade's work, Alec Cairncross, noted Oxford economist, predicts that the state will ultimately be obliged to moderate the bargaining advantages currently enjoyed by the trade unions.

Lionel [Lord] Robbins, professor emeritus of economics at the London School of Economics, formerly relying on demand-pull explanations of inflation, shifted his position markedly in an article appearing in *The Financial Times,* London, June 23, 1971. Similarly, his colleague, Frank W. Paish, in the second edition of his *Rise and Fall of Incomes Policy* (London: Institute of Economic Affairs, 1971), long skeptical of wage controls, concluded that the United Kingdom was confronted with a cost-push so serious as to call for a compulsory incomes policy. In fact, he added a postscript in the 1971 edition on incomes policies entitled "Cost-Push at Last."

While Paish is still largely preoccupied with Keynesian fiscal policies, and to a lesser extent with monetary policies, he reluctantly notes that direct control over wages may be inevitable. Previous incomes policies, he states, were concerned with conditions of excess demand. "Their failure," he says, "provides no indication of the probable result of a similar attempt made now, when the excess of demand for labor has been eliminated and its sole purpose would be to restrain the use of the monopoly power by labor."

---

18. James E. Meade, *Wages and Prices in a Mixed Economy* (London: Institute of Economic Affairs, 1971), pp. 18-19. This and other IEA studies quoted by permission.

Even so, his main concern is still with revised or more potent fiscal and monetary measures, which, he seems to think, can restrain the unions without generating rising unemployment. The logic is difficult to follow. But, finally, he does discuss, in a few sentences, direct limitations on wage increases and he advises study of proposed tax increases on employers making payments in excess of the govern-ment-prescribed norm. Government might also consider giving financial assistance to employers who suffer losses from strikes called to enforce wage claims in excess of a government norm. Paish admits that to make the wage restraint palatable, price controls might have to be resorted to—though, on strict economic grounds, he sees no argument for them under the stated conditions of economic slack.

In short, economists both from here and abroad, who are regarded as objective analysts, share the view that wage-push inflation is a reality and calls for labor-union restraint if the public interest is to be preserved.

## SOME DISSENTS FROM THE WAGE-PUSH

Still, there are some outstanding economists who reject the wage-push theory. Dr. Allan Meltzer of Carnegie-Mellon University insists that the only way to control inflation is via fiscal and monetary policy. (*The Wall Street Journal,* February 15, 1972.)

Possibly the most serious case against wage-push was made by Dr. George P. Shultz, formerly dean of the graduate School of Business at the University of Chicago, labor arbitrator, secretary of labor beginning in 1969, the first director of the reorganized Office of Management and Budget (successor to the Bureau of the Budget in the executive branch of the national bureaucracy), and in 1972 secretary of the treasury. (His credentials are worth noting in some detail because Dr. Shultz was highly influential in Washington as one of the two or three closest economic advisers to President Nixon from 1969 through 1972.)

The March 1970 issue of *Nation's Business* carried an illuminating article titled "George Shultz: General Manager of the United States." Here he is quoted as saying that the government's role is to provide a mix of fiscal and monetary policy that encourages growth with stability. In such a climate, he said, bad decisions in the private sector bring their own penalties—a greedy management prices itself out of the market, a greedy union prices itself out of jobs.

Did Dr. Shultz mean that error in management brings its own penalty to the point where we should abandon antitrust policy and save the taxpayers and shareholders a lot of money? Does Dr. Shultz think that John L. Lewis worried about shrinking employment in the coal mines, so long as he could collect sizable dues from the remaining members? Does Dr. Shultz really think that union officials are interested in maximizing jobs? He was the last strong hold-out against the freeze, although some 93 percent of business economists polled in late summer 1971 favored some form of freeze, despite their preference in principle for free-market decision-making. [19]

But there is a fundamental error in Shultz's analysis, as shown by Charles H. Smith, Jr., chairman of Sifco Industries, Inc. in the May 1970 issue of *Nation's Business.* Smith noted that a bad decision on prices by management tends to be largely self-correcting before it becomes fatal to the enterprise and its employees, but when a union forces a decision on wages—which fits the definition of "greedy"— the suggested penalty of a loss of jobs occurs only after management and investors have been penalized—when the enterprise has lost a significant portion of the market, or has been forced out of business.

Bad labor contracts are largely *irreversible.* Smith points out how helpless management is in the face of the massive monopoly power of labor unions, and the insignificance of the penalties imposed on them if they exploit that power to the full:

> It has been said that if such dire results can be expected from a "greedy" contract, management should have the wisdom not to agree to the contract. The point that most men in our government fail to recognize is that monopoly powers have been given to unions that enable them to force management to agree to demands whether they are unreasonable or not.
>
> A strike can stop production and bring serious economic

---

19. *Business Economics,* January 1972, p. 87ff.

consequences to the enterprise immediately. A picket line can prevent the replacement of strikers.

Brute force can intimidate those who might desire to pass through a picket line.

While the company or enterprise is struggling with the consequences of such a work stoppage, those manning the picket line are provided with strike benefits often raised from voluntary and involuntary contributions of the employees of competing firms. When the strike is considered to be important enough to organized labor, the strike benefit funds might come from thousands of different sources that have nothing really to do with the employer or the strike issue.

Government actually subsidizes the strikers, Smith pointed out, further unbalancing the scales:

In other words, the disciplines of the free market do not work to force the correction of "bad" or "greedy" decisions made by unions until serious harm has been done first to the enterprise, its management and owners, and to the economy of the country.

Actually, in many cases, "correction" is never made. Union officials don't admit error, since their primary aim is to maximize not total wages, but rather the wages of those who remain in employment.

After a new, expensive contract is wrung from a company (the consumer), the union official may call a press conference and announce that this is the largest and best contract ever signed by the union. Never once, over a period of more than a generation in observing union behavior, have I noted a single public statement by a union official recognizing the disemployment effects of extravagant contract settlements. The seniority clause in most union contracts generally tends to protect the majority of union members from prompt disemployment due to excessive wage settlements. The consumer does not vote the union boss into office; the union official knows who does—and he acts accordingly.

Clearly, Dr. Shultz—even though he specialized in labor economics and acted as arbitrator in labor disputes—had not grasped the realities of "free" collective bargaining. Charles H. Smith, Jr. is not merely a victim of "imported rising costs," as Friedman might suggest. He is a close student of the problem. In addition to a long industrial career, he has served on numerous private and government labor-advisory boards and commissions, and has for many years been the official employer delegate to the International Labor Office (ILO) in Switzerland, where he has exchanged experiences with economists and labor, government and industrial delegates from all over the world, including the Communist countries (the Communist representation causes George Meany to urge our government to withhold contributions to the ILO).

Smith's analysis in *Nation's Business* has done a great deal to clarify matters. Cost-push under tight money, causes unemployment; this in turn tends to foster deficit spending and loose monetary policy. In the first eight months of 1971, for example, the money supply was increased at a rate of 10 to 12 percent, which was highly inflationary, to overcome the sluggishness of the economy. This sluggishness was, to a large but undetermined degree, due to the wage-push. Union officials rarely oppose government spending, and show little concern over deficit spending by the government.

Friedman has been the chief challenger of wage-push as a cause of inflation; yet more than twenty years ago he came close to recognizing its reality:

> ... at least for the near future ... the difficulty is not so much that strong unions will produce inflation as that inflation will produce strong unions. Inflation ... will mean rising money-wage rates throughout the economy. Wherever unions exist or are created, the rises in wage rates ... will take place through the medium of the unions, and the unions will receive credit for the wage rises. This will tend to strengthen the hold of the unions on the workers and greatly to increase their political power. ...
>
> If the process just sketched should occur it would tend to change the balance of forces and perhaps ultimately to justify the fear that strong unions will produce inflation. For as the inflation proceeded, the rigidity effect of unions would tend to become weaker relative to their upward-pressing effects. ... [20]

---

20. Friedman, *The Impact of the Union.* Edited by David M. Wright (New York: Harcourt Brace, 1951), p. 230. This was one of the first scholarly compendiums by noted students on the power of unions to cause inflation.

Of course, Friedman has never denied that a union can drive up wages and force price increases in a particular plant or industry; monopoly power in the market must have some economic effects. But this is not what is meant by inflation—even though many people see every price increase—particularly increases they dislike—as inflation. But inflation, more accurately, usually means a rise over a period of time in some general index of prices, such as the Consumer or the Wholesale Price Index. Individual prices and wages should not remain rigid, but should adjust to market forces, so we need some broader measure by which to define inflation.

Most analysts reject the naive wage-price spiral argument, which holds, for example, that negotiated increases in particular wage rates produce increases in particular prices and, consequently, inflation, without regard to what is happening in other areas of the economy or to the fiscal and monetary policy and the supply of money. If the supply or velocity of money is not increased after substantial wage and price increases in some industry or sector, the result will not be an inflationary wage-price spiral. Rather, unemployment is likely to ensue, with reduced output along with higher prices (depending upon price elasticity) in the sector in which the wage-push has occurred. But this tends to be accompanied by downward pressures on wages and prices in the rest of the economy and increases in employment and output there. Thus, even if a substantial sector of the economy is unionized and subsequent large wage increases lead to price increases, this sequence *by itself* need not set in motion a wage-price spiral across the economy.

Friedman puts it this way:

> The existence of a strong union in one area simply means that wage rates in that area will be *higher* relative to wage rates elsewhere, and employment in that area *lower* relative to employment elsewhere than wages and employment would have been in the absence of a union. It does not mean that there will be pressure for these differentials to *widen.* Yet it is the latter that is required to produce the sequence embodied in the sophisticated wage-price spiral argument. *Increasingly strong* unions not simply strong unions are a necessary (though not sufficient) condition

108

for setting the wage-price spiral in motion. The failure to recognize this distinction is an example of one of the most prevalent fallacies in theorizing about economic events, a fallacy that arises in many other contexts in which "high" is confused with "rising" and "low" with "falling." A "high" price will generally have a very different effect than a "rising" price. . . .[21]

If the wage-price push creates substantial unemployment, and public authorities are induced to employ public measures (spending, tax cutting, credit ease) to remedy the situation, then it could be properly argued that the combination of circumstances and events produced, or paved the way for, inflation.

As Friedman puts it:

We all recognize that a more sophisticated theory can be formulated that is acceptable. This more sophisticated version requires that the monetary authorities or monetary and fiscal authorities be committed to "full-employment" and proceed to take expansionary measures, including expanding the money supply at more than the rate consistent with stable prices, whenever and however unemployment rises above some minimum level. Under such circumstances, it is certainly logically possible for an autonomous wage-push which would produce unemployment if the money supply were not changed in response to it to be converted into an inflationary spiral by the expansionary monetary policy it generates. . . .

That was Friedman in 1958. In his *Newsweek* column of September 28, 1970, he took an exceptionally uncompromising position against the wage-push and cost-push theories generally; possibly space limitations explain the apparent switch. The earlier and more sophisticated view is the correct one, in that it provides a truer prediction of future events in the real world of politics and pressures, and a more realistic prescription for warding off inflation.

---

21. Milton Friedman, Industrial Relations Research Association, *Annual Proceedings,* "Discussion," December 1958; p. 213.

## ECONOMIC DISTORTIONS

This chapter has been concerned primarily with the labor union and inflation. In the volume as a whole, however, the emphasis has been on other economic distortions of coercive collective bargaining. Union officials rarely cooperate with employers to tackle the accumulated featherbedding and uneconomic work practices. It was only after blue-collar jobs with the three major tire manufacturers in Akron, Ohio, dropped from 52,000 in 1944 to 14,000 in 1971 that the unions agreed to help eliminate the obstacles to the retention of the rubber-tire plants in the city.[22]

Union officials have yet to show any similar concern for the imbalance in our international payments, though their responsibility there may be equally great. By the beginning of the 1970s, numerous union officials had switched from tolerance of freer international trade and investment to extreme hostility.[23]

Despite their outpouring of articles, pamphlets, and books on almost every conceivable subject, economists have been singularly quiet on distortions, wage rigidities, and featherbedding.[24] (Burns and Haberler do stress the importance of improving the labor market and reducing union power.)

Likewise, no formal study has been made of the position of labor unions and their federations on government spending, deficit spending, the monetization of the public debt; nor of their opposition to sharing the burden of financing the enlarged government outlays that they urge and that their upward wage pressures make necessary; responsible monetary and fiscal policies are not urged by union officials.

Meanwhile, in several following chapters we examine further into the massive power of the union officials and their organizations.

---

22. *Business Week*, 12 February 1972, p. 44.

23. Ibid., p. 14.

24. Academicians, in examining unions and union policy positions, often seem to be misled by union slogans and resolutions. See, for example, Robert Lekachman and Brendan Sexton, "Papers and Proceedings," *American Economic Review,* May 1972.

# THE ROLE
# OF VIOLENCE IN
# COLLECTIVE BARGAINING

Violence in collective bargaining has come to mean the use of physical force, or the threat thereof, usually against employers, though it may also be used against employees, consumers, suppliers, and distributors. At times the threat may be psychological, or implicit, as in the case of a threatening midnight telephone call. Violence is most frequent during strikes, but it may also occur during unionizing campaigns. The strike as the lever of union power generally involves two steps: (1) employees stop work in unison and (2) other workers are prevented from competing for the jobs, usually on any terms, but particularly on terms inferior to those sought by the striking union. If the union were unable to prevent other applicants from taking their jobs, the strike would be no more than a mass resignation.

## UNAWARENESS OF VIOLENCE

It follows that violence and the threat of violence are an integral part of collective bargaining. Union officials insist that the unions' "ultimate weapon" is the strike. But this is not true. The ultimate weapon is violence—either actual, or pending, or threatened. Though overt force, coercion, and violence are absent when a union demand is made, their availability and potential use are always there, day by day, and hour by hour. They are there when a strike vote is taken, when a strike is threatened, when a strike is called. The full impact of force and violence cannot be measured by their actual and overt employment. That is why so few people are even aware of union violence, or of its chilling effect on the employer.

Union officials, and some politicians, at times in high dudgeon, defend "labor's right to strike," but they rarely if ever point out that to be effective, the unions must be able to prevent—by force, if necessary—the hiring of other workers to take their place.

Mass picketing and boycotts—primary and secondary—may be employed to put pressure on the employer. Secondary boycotts (against the struck employer's suppliers or vendors, for example) are generally illegal, yet they go on, and they do their damage, until stopped—by which time they may have brought the employer to heel. Mass picketing is virtually always illegal. But by the time countermeasures are taken, it, too, may have had its intended effect, and as Chamberlin points out, the strike "settlement" will include forgiving all illegal conduct in the interest of "harmonious relationships." Physical violence is everywhere regarded as illegal, but this does not stop its extensive use.

Today, when a plant is struck, the employer generally makes no attempt to keep it running. A few pickets at each entrance bear signs notifying other employees and the customers of the facts of life. The employer's apparent supineness follows from his knowledge that he cannot get injunctive relief for anticipated damages or financial losses.

If the employer tries to keep his establishment operating, some of the employees may stay on the job, other workers may take jobs, and, in time, a back-to-work movement among the strikers may begin. This may terminate the strike in fact, while it goes on "officially" for months and even years. The January 1963 strike against the Florida East Coast Railway Company was not "called off" until January 1972.

To avoid a breach of the peace, the police may permit pickets to block entry and may refuse to help nonunion employees or union employees not wanting to strike, to cross the line. This is another way of saying that the police support the picket line. John V. Lindsay, the mayor of New York City, has never really tried to enforce freedom and order in strikes along the city's waterfronts.

During the strike against the General Electric Company in 1969, local government officials actually pleaded with nonunion workers to refrain from crossing picket lines. Union newspapers, pamphlets, and other printed material, including some issued by the AFL-CIO, repeatedly stress the advantage of labor's influence with "city hall," including the office of the chief of police.

## DATA ON VIOLENCE

No comprehensive or systematic study of the use of violence during organizing campaigns and during strikes has been made in the United States, although thousands of episodes, some very serious, have been reported in the press over the years. Labor economists in the universities have shown little interest in this aspect of unionism. A letter addressed to the Institute of Labor and Industrial Relations at a major state university in November 1971 brought this rather remarkable response from the managing editor of the publication office of the Institute:

> We do not have any material dealing with union violence
> or with related areas, and I am afraid that no one here was
> able to suggest anywhere that you might even look.

A lengthy, somewhat impressionistic review of strikes is available in *Violence in America,* a report made in 1969 to the National Commission on the Causes and Prevention of Violence.[1]

Professors Philip Taft and Philip Ross prepared the section on labor violence (Chapter VIII). They recognize that considerable violence is unreported and unrecorded, *but how much is unknown.* Based on cases handled by the National Labor Relations Board (NLRB) and its regional offices, they estimate that some eighty to one hundred cases of unlawful acts, with some degree of violence committed by labor unions, occurred in 1968. The nature and extent of the violence is not discussed. Whether a few or hundreds of other cases occurred in that year is not known.

---

1. *The History of Violence in America* (Washington, D.C. Government Printing Office, 1969). Also published by F. A. Praeger, New York.

Possibly because of time and space limitations, the authors give us virtually no analysis of or statistics on the violence in such fairly recent major cases as the strikes against the Kohler Company, the Kingsport Press, Southern Bell Telephone, Florida East Coast Railway Company, Perfect Circle, or the Louisville and Nashville Railroad—to name a few. The authors lament the lack of data on the frequency and intensity of violence. Cases handled locally and not coming to the attention of the NLRB or the Department of Justice may go unrecorded. The authors contacted some local police departments, the FBI, and other sources, but they admit that time limitations prevented "any intensive collection of data."

## STRIKE ENFORCEMENT
## VERSUS EMPLOYER'S RIGHT TO OPERATE

Professors Taft and Ross strongly condemn violence in strike situations, while recognizing its ever-present potential: "Violence on a picket line is always latent but tends to surface when the employer recruits replacements and attempts to operate." Employers, they note, have the legal right to move goods and people freely across the picket line, and the duty and practice of police has tended to safeguard this right.

They applaud the recent reduction in violence, without considering the possibility that the decline may have been bought at an excessive price: settlements that have disrupted the smooth functioning of the economy, augmented inflation, and exacerbated the imbalance of international payments. Thus, strikes and the threats of strikes have created a serious, possibly insoluble, dilemma for the two parties, management and unions, and for society as a whole.

A strike, however legal, will be ineffective if the employer exercises his legal rights and succeeds in keeping his establishment operating effectively and profitably. So the union officials, in their own interest, must block operations. How to solve this dilemma? Considering the damage done to society as a whole by strikes and the attendant violence, it would seem that the employer's interests coincide with society's more nearly than do the union officials'.

114

Governments in the United States, although often favoring unionization and the so-called right to strike, have not explicitly sanctioned the use of violence by either unions or management. Mass picketing and violence are illegal. The problem is the enforcement of laws that *totally* eliminate the practices. Then the problems of unionism would largely wither away, even though the privilege of joining a union could be preserved.

Taft and Ross credit the NLRB with the great reduction in union violence. Elsewhere, they tell us that local law-enforcement agencies are able, with rare exceptions, to keep the peace. In another report Philip Taft says that laws, such as the Wagner Act of 1935, compelling employers to recognize unions representing their employees in a proper bargaining unit, have perhaps been the primary cause for a lessening of violence in labor disputes.[2] Professor Sylvester Petro, on the other hand, comes to a contrary conclusion. He is most critical of the behavior of the NLRB, particularly in cases of union violence against *workers*.[3] He shows that the NLRB has failed to enforce the *law which requires that unions reimburse workers for pay lost due to the use of violence.* For years the NLRB denied that it had such power. Petro, citing law and cases, shows that unions may not legally threaten nonstrikers with any form of physical injury or reprisal. They may not injure or threaten to injure employees who for one reason or another refuse to become members, or members who choose to continue working during a strike.

The Taft-Hartley Act (Section 10 (j) ) gave the NLRB power to seek, and the federal courts power to grant, injunctive relief against unfair practices, whether committed by union or employer. Never once, says Petro, had the Board used this power to make a union pay an employee either for physical injury or loss of employment caused by its violence. Petro, with painstaking research and documentation, shows that the Board's disclaimer regarding its power to order reimbursement is in error. He says the only "remedy" fashioned by

---

2. Philip Taft, "Violence in American Labor Disputes," *The Annals of the Academy of Political and Social Science,* Philadelphia, Pa., March 1966.

3. Sylvester Petro, *How the NLRB Can Stop Union Violence* (Washington, D.C.: Labor Policy Association, 1958).

the NLRB in union-violence cases has been a mere cease-and-desist order, usually issued long after the violence has occurred, "a meaningless gesture which cannot possibly do anything to effectuate the policies of the Act."

## STATES' POLICE POWER

The courts have consistently held that the use of police power to prevent violence, destruction of property, and other disorders in labor disputes, remains an inalienable power of the states, despite the extensive federal regulation in this field.[4]

Contradictory court decisions and the vacillation of the U. S. Supreme Court have, however, extended confusion to state and local authorities, including courts, governors, mayors, and police departments. Many state and local measures to stop violence have been criticized, enjoined, and overturned. This has encouraged uncertainty, vacillation, and hesitation at the state and local levels.

Were problems of law and order and union violence left entirely to the several states, the enlightened self-interest of the citizens of the states would act as a natural disciplining force; in the states and communities where the laws and ordinances against force and violence are inadequate or inadequately enforced, new investments in job-making facilities would be increasingly difficult to attract. Existing enterprises might migrate, or might hesitate to expand in their present location, thus creating unemployment and forcing youngsters and others to migrate in search of adequate job opportunities. This need for new job-making investments can be an exceptionally effective natural restraint on the use of force and violence. But centralization of authority in remote Washington has greatly reduced its usefulness. States with "right-to-work" laws frequently advertise the fact in the national press as an inducement to plants and other establishments to locate within their boundaries.

---

4. Gerard D. Reilly in *State Rights and the Law of Labor Relations* (Washington, D.C., American Enterprise Institute, 1958), analyzes the areas of conflict between the two layers of government, and reveals a mass of wandering and inconsistent court findings, including those of the U. S. Supreme Court itself.

## HOW SERIOUS IS VIOLENCE NOW?

Violence appears to have declined, but appearances may be deceiving. Prior to compulsory recognition of unions, coercion and violence seemed to be exercised largely by employers and were front-page news. Now that most employers have ceded their right to continue operations, union officials know how to gain their ends without resort to overt violence and thus avoid brushes with the law. Consequently the public is less aware than in earlier days of the prevalence of violence. Even so, it is still extensive, almost invariably breaking out whenever an employer attempts to keep operating, or when two unions are engaged in jurisdictional fights. But coming from the side of labor, it rarely gets the attention that the violence of earlier days attracted.

One noted legal scholar in this field has told me that there are as many items, cases, and instances involving union violence in his files as there are on any other subject in the area of labor law and industrial relations. Proof by anecdote may not be persuasive, yet anyone could make a long list. Or the recent study by Johnson and Kotz, mentioned in Chapter I, could be consulted.

Only recently (February 1, 1972) *The Evening Star* of Washington reported the personal appeal of Governor Marvin Mandel of Maryland to the head of the Baltimore Building and Construction Council "to help cool" what appeared to be *a growing pattern of violence against nonunion contractors.* Fires had disrupted work on Towson State College's $6,000,000 fine arts building and seven persons had been arrested. Earlier disturbances had occurred at sites at Morgan State College and at the Keswick Home for Incurables, both in Baltimore.

A few days later the same paper made the following report:

> Two weeks ago union pickets suddenly began appearing outside nonunion construction projects and violence followed.
>
> At Morgan State College, two nonunion men were beat up and a shed was set afire near a library under construction.

117

At Towson State College, a trailer and crane were burned at the campus's new $6,000,000 fine arts building. Pickets blocked firemen from easy access to the blaze.

At a nursing home project in the city, two construction trailers were burned and a crane was fire-bombed.

Next to the Bromo Seltzer Tower downtown, two non-union workers and two policemen were beat up as officers tried to escort laborers through pickets to a pumping station under construction.

In all, twenty-seven men were arrested, most of them on disorderly conduct charges.

When violence occurs, what actually takes place? Let us look at a few cases, the first going back more than twenty years.

In July 1951, some four thousand employees, members of the Teamsters' Union in New York City and its suburbs, struck sixteen large bakeries. The action cut off 80 percent of bread deliveries, but this did not affect the smaller "independent" bakeries. "So the strike did not pinch the public much, and that made the teamsters angry," *Time* of July 16, 1951, reported. It went on to state:

> Soon, though the independent drivers themselves are members of the Teamsters' Union, roving goon squads formed menacingly around the nonstriking bakeries, blocked off the highways and bridges leading out of town. Bricks were heaved through windshields, drivers slapped and pummeled, tires punctured, ignition systems ripped out, sugar poured into gas tanks. Drivers from bakeries not involved in the strike were forced off the road; one lost $480 in receipts, others watched helplessly while their loads of bread, pies and cakes were trampled, fouled with chemicals, strewn along the streets. At one bakery, 100 shouting pickets kept 45 trucks from moving. By week's end many of the nonstriking drivers had decided to stay at home, independent bakeries had stopped deliveries, and New York City and its suburbs were out of bread. All that federal mediators could report was no progress.

This is an example of what can happen when some employers, or a part of an industry, stays in operation when a strike is called.

The typical union official is often intolerant of dissenting view among workers. Emil Mazey, vice president of the United Auto

118

mobile Workers and second in command after the late Walter Reuther, said, with regard to the Kohler strike, "No one has a right to scab *despite the law.*"[5] (Italics supplied.)

Petro analyzed the forty volumes of McClellan hearings and published his findings in a highly enlightening book, *Power Unlimited— The Corruption of Union Leadership.* He stated that Mazey

> ... and other UAW officials, made it perfectly clear that, in their opinion, the nonstrikers were outlaws against whom any kind of reprisal would be no more than they had earned. According to Mazey, if a majority of employees vote to strike, it is exactly the same as when Congress votes to go to war. On one occasion when he made such a comparison, Chairman McClellan caught him up:
>
> "We are not talking about war. We are talking about the right of an individual to make a decision to follow a livelihood for himself or his family."
>
> When Mazey said, "There is a great deal of similarity, Senator," the Chairman responded with:
>
> "I do not think so. I think a man who has a job, who wants to go to work, should have the right. I think you should have the right to strike and you should have a right to put those pickets out there ... but you do not have any right to mass them in front of that gate where a man who wants to work cannot get in."
>
> Mazey's supremely arrogant response to this clean statement of law and morality was: "You have a right to your opinion and I have a right to my opinion. . . ."[6]

Petro summed up many years of study:

> The present power of trade unions stems largely from special privileges that the government has conferred— notably the union shop and the exclusive bargaining status that unions gain when they command a bare majority of employees in a plant. The greatest abuse of unions today is

---

5. *Hearings of the Select Committee on Improper Activities in the Labor or Management Field,* 85th Congress, 2nd Session, or, for short, the *McClellan Committee Hearings,* p. 8980.

6. New York, N.Y.: Ronald Press, 1959.

their widespread exercise of force—overt or covert—on American workers and employers. . . .[7]

The last sentence may come as a shock, or at least as a surprise, to some who have not followed these matters very closely.

In a study of the United Automobile Workers' strike of the 1950s against the Kohler Company, Petro discovered that massive violence and coercion had been employed and condoned by unions—including the international union officials. He said:

> As soon as mass picketing was prevented by an injunction, a campaign of violence and vandalism started. A non-striker's telephone might ring at intervals all night. If he picked it up he would hear threats and obscenities. In the morning his car's paint might be ruined by acid, or sugar in his gasoline tank might put the engine out of commission. A "paint bomb" might be hurled through a window of his house and shatter against the wall, ruining rugs and furniture. His livestock might sicken, and investigation would reveal that they had been poisoned. A count placed the number of such incidents at more than 400, but the count was limited to those who came forward with affidavits, and it is therefore probably low.[8]

Many other references to violence and vandalism are to be found throughout the pages of Petro's volume. In a volume on the strike against Kingsport Press, which started in March 1963, Petro reported more than one thousand acts of violence and coercion. Much permanent damage was done to workers and their families.[9]

One union organizer in the coal fields said in disgust, "We didn't have organizers. We had men who went in with a stick of dynamite in one hand and a shotgun in the other. They just terrorized people into paying royalties and into joining the union."[10]

---

7. *Fortune,* November 1959.

8. *The Kohler Strike: Union Violence and Administrative Law* (Chicago: Regnery Co., 1961).

9. *The Kingsport Strike* (New Rochelle, N.Y., Arlington House, 1967).

10. *Fortune,* January 1971, article by Thomas O'Hanlon on "Anarchy Threatens the Kingdom of Coal." See also *Wall Street Journal* editorial on the massive violence in construction in Philadelphia area, September 5, 1972.

Charles Minton, who testified in the murder case of Joseph A. Yablonski—who had dared run against Tony Boyle for the presidency of the United Mine Workers in 1969—brought suit against the union and swore that he had dynamited mine installations on union orders, but had balked when Boyle ordered him to kill C. P. Fugate and Harry Turner, two nonunion coal operators. Minton claimed that Boyle promised a substantial reward if he carried out the assignment, and legal assistance and aid to his family if he was apprehended. The case was settled out of court and Boyle (successor to John L. Lewis as President of UMW) would not comment on the matter.[11] In 1972, the UMW election of 1969 was set aside because of the illegal and fraudulent actions that had been taken by the union officers. The president was sentenced to jail, fined $130,000, and ordered to repay the union funds that he had improperly spent for political purposes.

Even though there is no overt violence in most strikes, potential violence hovers in the background as the ultimate weapon. During the 1959 steel strike, numerous commentators and writers, unaware of the reasons for the quiet on the picket lines, applauded the absence of violence. Nevertheless, *The New York Times* (August 6, 1959) reported the use of force:

> A siege was lifted today for 267 supervisory employees at the United States Steel Company's Fairless works. . . . The nonunion workers had been inside the plant since the steel strike began on July 14th. . . . Late last night the 267 headed home for the first time in more than three weeks. . . . From now on the supervisory personnel will be allowed to enter and leave the plant at will for maintenance.

On July 13, 1971, the Richmond, Va., *News Leader* published accounts of sixty-five separate acts of violence, coercion, and discomfort against its employees, offering a financial reward to anyone providing information that would lead to the arrest and conviction of anyone guilty of assault, malicious damage, etc. Herewith are the first ten of these items, and the last six.

---

11. *Fortune,* ibid.

## 1. APRIL 13, 1971

Splotches of dried spittle found all over windshield and body of car parked near Mechanical Building of Richmond Newspapers.

## 2. APRIL 14, 1971

Eggs broken on truck and rear lights of car parked near Mechanical Building.

## 3. APRIL 15, 1971

Delivery truck driver reported he was followed by two men in a car who, after he had made a stop, tried to get a policeman to charge him with hit and run. Officer refused because of no injury or damage. A charge of reckless driving was next attempted but charge was dismissed by the court.

## 4. APRIL 15, 1971

Another employee reported eggs and spittle on car.

## 5. APRIL 17, 1971

Three or four pounds of roofing nails were found at Third and Fourth street entrances to Mechanical Building, with four flat tires reported on delivery trucks. Still another flat was reported at night from roofing nails.

## 6. APRIL 17, 1971

Still more roofing nails were found in parking lot and near company garage—three or four pounds in all.

122

## 7. APRIL 18, 1971

Woman employee, leaving work at 2 o'clock at night, reported that on two previous nights she had been followed by men who took her license number and on one occasion followed her to her home.

## 8. APRIL 19, 1971

Woman employee in the composing room, on a temporary basis, reported that she parked her car the night before on Fourth between Grace and Franklin and upon leaving her job at midnight found that her car had been sprayed with paint from one end to the other.

## 9. APRIL 26, 1971

News rack in front of the Reynolds Building was vandalized, with cement glue being placed in the coin mechanism. Replacement of parts necessary.

## 10. APRIL 29, 1971

A Composing Room employee, living in Chesterfield, found his car's gasoline tank had been filled with sugar during the night while at home. Replacement of the tank was necessary.

## 60. JULY 5, 1971

Employee reported that right rear panel window on his station wagon had been shot out, while parked at home.

## 61. JULY 6, 1971

Employee reported that rear window and a side window shattered by shots that apparently were not noticed in July 4 weekend noise.

## 62. JULY 7, 1971

Employee, "visited" before, this time was sleeping on his porch when he heard two shots at 2:34 A.M. Shots apparently aimed at his car, which he had tried to camouflage with heavy plastic. Shots missed target and he observed a car roar off.

## 63. JULY 7, 1971

Employee reported that his car had been damaged on four occasions, with latest occurring during firecracker celebrations. At the time, explosions did not alarm him; later, he discovered rear window shattered and windshield badly punctured.

## 64. JULY 8, 1971

Employee reported that he had been awakened by police at 1:30 A.M., who had been called by a neighbor. Neighbor had heard noise as employee's windshield was being smashed, apparently with a hammer. The rear panel window, previously smashed and then repaired, once more was smashed in addition to the windshield.

## 65. JULY 8, 1971

Employee reported damage that had occurred over the holiday weekend, when eggs were thrown against his house at 1:40 A.M., July 5. He was awake at time, kept watch a while, and when a car later returned he showed himself and it roared off.

Up to late 1971 at least, no acts of violence had been directed at the employer or its properties.[12]

---

12. (Letter from a company officer, and discussed with an editor.) Material reprinted with permission of the publisher.

For those who think violence does not occur any more in "our enlightened age," a careful study of these sixty-five acts would be illuminating. Unless one lived in the Richmond area or subscribed to the Richmond papers, knowledge of this vandalism would most likely be nil.

In January 1963, a number of nonoperating railway unions struck the Florida East Coast Railway Company, which has nearly six hundred miles of road. The strike continued until it was the longest rail strike in our history, finally terminating in 1972. *Barron's* analyzed the issues and events in a series of articles.[13] It reported: "In a shattering campaign of harassment, intimidation, train-derailing, arson, and dynamiting, which reached a climax in February and March 1964, they subjected the FEC to over 300 acts of sabotage and other violence." (April 12 issue.)

At the end of the first day of a strike in July 1971, by the Communications Workers of America against the American Telephone and Telegraph Company, *The Wall Street Journal* (July 15, 1971), with no claim of comprehensive coverage, reported:

> Telephone company vehicles were said to have been turned over in Scarsdale and Greenburgh, N.Y., and cars entering a Western Electric parking lot in Buffalo, N.Y., were said to have been damaged and their drivers harassed by pickets.
>
> In some areas in Pennsylvania and Ohio, supervisory personnel said they were unable to get through picket lines at local offices, and the company threatened to seek court injunctions against the pickets if they continued the alleged obstruction of nonstrikers into telephone offices and arrested two pickets for alleged threats.
>
> Other reports said 20 pickets were arrested in Broward County, Fla., for blocking company offices, that vandals in the Miami area cut a news agency cable and burned cables serving 230 customers and that six pickets were arrested in Newark, N.J., after policemen were spattered with eggs. In Hollywood, Calif., telephone supervisors told police that pickets had thrown lighted flares at their cars.

---

13. *Barron's,* New York, May 11 and 18, 1964, and April 12, 1965. Reprints of these articles are available from the railway company, St. Augustine, Florida.

At Cape Kennedy, Fla., strikers picketed two entrances to the space center, but government officials said the dispute wouldn't have any effect on the countdown rehearsal in progress for the July 26 Apollo 15 launching of the 15th U. S. moon shot.

One day later, another newspaper reported that widening vandalism had interrupted phone service for thousands of Americans as the Communication Workers of America strike against the Bell System entered its third day. Equipment reportedly was cut and burned in Illinois, South Carolina, California, and New York, leaving large areas without phone service. The worst damage was north of Chicago, where lines were cut, a garage was fire-bombed and office windows were smashed. The Illinois Bell Telephone Company announced it was cutting off talks with the International Brotherhood of Electrical Workers because of what it called "vicious and insane" acts of violence. The IBEW, which represented some non-CWA phone workers, was not on strike. Damage was estimated at $100,000 by the company.

In Westchester County, north of New York City, cut lines left about 3,200 customers without service, the telephone company reported. About 1,500 were without phones because lines were cut in the San Fernando Valley outside Los Angeles, phone officials said. Nonstriking workers were evacuated from an office in New Rochelle, New York, after a sulphur bomb was thrown into a ventilating system.

A company supervisor reportedly was beaten in Yonkers, New York, while doing repairs, and a policeman was shoved through a plate-glass window by pickets in Cleveland as nonstrikers were being escorted to work. In Pennsylvania, five restraining orders were put into effect to keep pickets from blocking entrances to phone company buildings.

A spokesman for the FBI said the Bureau would have no comment on vandalism or other damage, other than to say it is investigating reports of such acts in South Carolina, Illinois, California, and New York (*Evening Star,* Washington, July 16, 1971).

An attempt was made to get accurate information on the violence in this telephone strike, but an officer of AT & T replied that this

126

would be in the hands of the subsidiary operating companies across the country, and they probably would not release the information! Why not?

These are only a few cases of union violence, mostly recent. Scores of others could be added. Yet, we have little information on the full scope, including known but isolated cases that do not make the newspapers, of the violence employed year after year. It does seem obvious that the reported cases are only a part of the story. Little is known about the scope and intensity, even of reported cases. When the strike ends, often "all is forgotten," partly because disgruntled union members can continue making costly mistakes, and otherwise punishing the employer.

There is a strong tendency among casual observers to seriously underestimate the role of violence in the collective bargaining process. Even Professor E. E. Witte, president of the American Economic Association in 1956 and a strong supporter of unionism, stated the case against violence but misinterpreted appearances. Note the words in italics:

> . . . preservation of law and order is a prime responsibility of government at all times, including periods of labor troubles.
> . . . there occasionally still is violence in labor disputes, but far less than in earlier years. *How much of the credit belongs to what government has done to preserve law and order and how much results from generally improved labor-management relations is debatable.* What is clear is that the preservation of law and order is an important function of which there can be no doubt whatsoever. . . .[14]

Taft and Ross assert that violence, ". . . could not be eliminated until its causes were removed." And ". . . violence will continue unless attention is paid to the removal of grievances." Given the nature of man and the politics within unionism, it is not clear what

---

14. Edwin E. Witte. "Government and Union-Management Relations: Past, Present, and Future," *Michigan Business Review,* Ann Arbor, Mich., November 1959, pp. 26-27.

the authors would regard as adequate removal of causes and elimination of grievances. Clearly union officials promote themselves by making massive demands; many union members like to view themselves as underpaid and overworked. The employer may fear insolvency if his costs get out of line with those of his competitors; he may try to operate during a strike in order to meet his commitments and remain solvent.

Employees and their employer have more common interests than antagonistic interests. Yet collective demands imposed on any one employer may expose him to intolerable competition from his domestic or foreign rivals. How then would Taft and Ross "remove the causes" or remove "the grievances," in order to eliminate violence?

Simons was well aware that surface tranquility may be deceptive; as long ago as 1944, he put the matter in these cogent words:

> Labor organization without large powers of coercion and intimidation is an unreal abstraction. Unions now have such powers; they always have had and always will have, so long as they persist in their present form. Where the power is small or insecurely possessed, it must be exercised overtly and extensively; large and unchallenged, it becomes like the power of strong government, confidently held, respectfully regarded, and rarely displayed conspicuously. [15]

Unlimited, unregulated power has, throughout history, proved to be too much for any person or group to exercise with equity, tolerance, and temperance. But two specific deficiencies tend to corrupt union leaders, although many of them come into unions with youthful idealism. One is in the kind of leaders attracted to or developed by any organization to which huge funds flow easily while necessary expenses are limited and hence on which no internal pressure to provide careful accounting is exerted (one reason why

---

15. "Some Reflections on Syndicalism," *Journal of Political Economy*. Chicago, Ill., University of Chicago Press, March 1944, p. 22. Professor Simons's article is one of the classics, with few peers, and merits rereading and wide circulation at this time. Also reproduced in his *Economic Policy for a Free Society* (Chicago, Ill.: University of Chicago Press, 1948).

politicians are tempted to permit license to be the order of the day ). The other is in the wide gap between the good theory and bad practice of too many of the union officials who are not misapropriating funds or directly corrupting politicians, but who act politically and economically against the genuine interests of the workers they are supposed to represent.

The interests of union officials are rarely identical with those of union members. Consequently, the members and the general public are frequently misinformed as to the real objectives of union policy. Proposals clearly against the interests of the members and the society as a whole are decked out in false colors, and accepted. This occurs because of the unwillingness of government agencies and the news media to scrutinize the proposals carefully, expose what their true effects will be, and point out that they may be the products of violence or the fear of violence so pervasive as to silence the few members who might otherwise have protested.

Public support of strong unions and collective bargaining, of strikes and violence, is due to the mistaken belief that workers cannot get "a fair shake" from employers unless the latter are virtually bludgeoned into making concessions. In a free labor market, wages and benefits tend to rise one step at a time, without fanfare or public announcement. If an employer wants to hold manpower and to recruit more of it, he must offer at least as good a deal as workers can get elsewhere. The employer is not free to exploit workers, nor to set remuneration to suit his own taste.

Unionized workers, on the other hand, get a pay increase often after much publicity, after strike threats or actual strikes, and possibly violence; thus the union *appears* to be delivering the higher pay. Politicians and others may conclude that without unions, workers' pay would be far lower than it now is.

Unions may alter *the timing* of wage changes without necessarily affecting the amount of change in a year, or over the longer pull. Unions do often get more for their members than the free market would pay, but over the longer pull, the spread between the non-unionized sectors and the unionized one has not widened. There is little, if any, evidence that unions raise wages for labor as a whole. As the unionized sector encompasses a larger proportion of the total work force, the impact of unionism on wages will be reduced; the real output determines what is available to workers and the other income claimants. If employers and the schools dispensed more economic education among their employees and students, they might greatly mitigate the propensity to strike and to engage in violence.[16]

The chasm between a legitimate theory of free collective bargaining and collective bargaining in practice is evidenced again by the AFL-CIO in "Collective Bargaining in America."[17] In this twelve-page, double-column explanation, there is only a casual and indirect reference to strikes, and none at all to union monopoly, to compulsory unionism and the use of force, nor to violence and coercion. It is like *Hamlet* minus the king of Denmark and the gravediggers. The pamphlet projects the image that union officials desire to convey to the public and if it were accurate, there might be no cause for complaint by management or the public. But its apparent innocence of the fact that something has gone astray with collective bargaining is just another example of the ease with which phantom word pictures can be painted.

Workers, capital, and entrepreneurship are necessary in any society. Unions are not, although if they are strictly voluntary and strictly nonviolent, they can be effective and useful instruments of communication with the public and with management.

If force, compulsion, coercion, and violence remain the instruments of the union movement, "the worst will come to the top," as F. V. Hayek predicted in *The Road to Serfdom.*[18]

Either unions will abandon violence, or unions will inevitably come under the extensive, exhaustive (and exhausting) control of the state. The late Lord Beveridge predicted in 1944, in his blueprint for the postwar welfare state, that if unions do not moderate their demands, wage determination "will perforce become a function of

---

16. An excellent example of what is needed is *The Truth About Boulwarism: Trying to Do Right Voluntarily* by Lemuel R. Boulware (Washington, D.C.: The Bureau of National Affairs, Inc.). Paperback, $2.95.

17. *Labor's Economic Review,* Washington, D.C., January 1960.

18. F. V. Hayek. *The Road to Serfdom* (Chicago, Ill.: University of Chicago Press, 1944).

the state." Unions and union officials have had their warning. It is not too late to act. George Meany and several presidents of international unions have suggested that the strike may be obsolete under current economic conditions.

Union officials carry a heavy share of the blame for the use of violence in industrial and labor relations; but government, whose primary and most basic function must always be the maintenance of law and order, has been enormously remiss in carrying out its responsibility.

For several decades students of the labor movement have persistently argued that once employers accept unions and do not challenge their survival, violence will subside and possibly disappear. This conclusion has some merit, but is not fully accurate by any means either here or abroad. *The Economist* (London, August 19, 1972) pointed out that construction contractors are seriously concerned about intimidation not only at the sites, but also directed at the men's wives and families. Although this type of picketing of a man's home was outlawed by the Industrial Labor Relations Act, "the militants do not worry about that" (p. 65). Violence and intimidation, *The Economist* reported, now accompany every major industrial dispute, (p. 21). The dock strike in 1972 involved massive coercion and violence.

# GOVERNMENT AID
# TO STRIKERS

The power of union officials and labor unions is augmented by governments at local, state, and national levels. The working man is taxed to subsidize the striker who decides not to work.

How quickly and how easily strikers may get onto welfare rolls is suggested by events in Allegheny County, Pennsylvania (Pittsburgh), when a steel strike was expected for August 1, 1971. A welfare official there said, "I just hate to think of it. It makes me pray for a miracle of no strike." To prepare for the expected deluge, he was considering setting up temporary welfare halls near the steel mills or at union headquarters. At least 250 staff persons would have to be added, he said, to process the claims anticipated from many of the nearly 60,000 steel workers in the county. The welfare agency, tax-supported, had been sending its agents to the union meetings to explain procedures and eligibility rules. No strike occurred.

In 1960, half a million steel workers were able to hold out for 116 days, thanks to about $45,000,000 in welfare and unemployment benefits from government sources. I. W. Abel, then secretary-treasurer of the Steel Workers Union, said candidly that the aid "provided food, shelter, and welfare services that made the strike endurable. The sum exceeded by far the amount that the union poured into the districts and the locals."[1]

---

1. From, *Here's the Issue,* Chamber of Commerce of USA, Washington, D.C., November 27, 1970, which carried other information reported herein. *The Wall Street Journal,* July 14, 1971 supplemented the above. See also the debate, "Should Strikers Be Denied Welfare Benefits?" (mimeographed) a Public Broadcasting Service program, December 14, 1971, Box 1971, Boston, Mass.: and *Welfare and Strikers: The Use of Public Funds to Support Strikes,* by Armand J. Thieblot and Ronald M. Cowin (Philadelphia, Pa.: University of Pennsylvania Press, Wharton School of Finance and Commerce, 1972).

William Rusher of *National Review* pointed out in a debate that the taxpayer thus pays twice: once for the welfare, and again in the higher prices that result from the higher costs the union imposes on the employer. He asked another participant in the debate, "Who suffers from this largess?" The answer was the taxpayer, the consumer who pays higher prices after the strike, and, finally, the really poor for whom there are reduced welfare funds, "unless you assume the welfare fund is a bottomless pit."

## DEVELOPMENT OF STRIKE SUBSIDIES

How did we get started on the policy of publicly financing strikes? The framers of our social security program in the mid-1930s wanted strike payments to be a part of the state unemployment-compensation systems. A number of states complied with the recommendation, but today only New York and Rhode Island retain the policy of paying strikers from benefits contributed entirely by the employers, after a few extra weeks of waiting.

The railways have, from the beginning, been covered by a separate system of social security. This includes a fully funded strike-benefit system paid for solely by employers, that is, by shippers and travelers. Under a 1938 law, railroad employees who participate in a legal strike, or who won't cross a picket line, or are prevented from working by a strike, are entitled to unemployment benefits. So employers are, in effect, forced to finance strikes against themselves.

AFL-CIO President George Meany insists that if railroad workers are denied the right to strike, the "government should seize and operate the railroads," as a matter of "simple justice," with the operating income turned over to the public treasury. But, one might ask, would there be any "operating income?" Not if government operation abroad is any indication of success.

The fact is that railroad workers *do* strike and *do* receive payments financed by the railroads for every day they are on strike. Since 1953, railroad employees on strike, or unemployed because of strikes, have received nearly $40,000,000 out of the Railroad Retirement insurance fund financed by employers (consumers). Decisions

134

of the Railroad Retirement Board granting benefits for unemployment resulting from a strike are not subject to judicial review at the request of the employer (who pays the cost), but an employee who is denied payment may obtain review.

The unfairness of employer-financed strike payments was cited by President Nixon in July 1969, when he asked Congress to strengthen the unemployment-compensation law for nonrailroad employees. "The unemployment tax we require employers to pay was never intended to supplement strike funds to be used against them," he said. "A worker who chooses to exercise his right to strike is not involuntarily unemployed." Calling attention to the strike-benefit laws in New York and Rhode Island, he said: "This is not the purpose of the unemployment insurance system."

In signing the legislation that ended a recent rail strike, the president pointed out that the wage increase without compensatory cost cuts was inflationary. The whole wage package had been deplored as inflationary by the Council of Economic Advisers in its *Inflation Alert.*

Actually, the payment of welfare benefits predates the 1930s. Families in need, largely regardless of the cause of the privation, have for many years been provided some help, mainly on the theory that mothers and children should not be made to suffer for faults not their own. This argument appeals to one's sense of justice, yet the policy undoubtedly results in more and longer strikes. If it is to be continued, the payments might, as *The Economist* has suggested, be made in the form of loans, not gifts. There is some precedent in the United Kingdom for loans instead of grants to people in need, and it would be a comparatively simple matter to inaugurate the policy in handling needy families of strikers.[2] It might reduce the number and duration of strikes and hence the tax burden and the wage-push.

All states have child-neglect laws. Should strikers escape the penalties provided by these laws, and then allow the child-support burden to be shifted to the taxpayer? In a letter to *The Wall Street Journal* (August 10, 1971) Clinton G. Knool stated:

---

2. *The Economist,* September 12, 1970.

All of our AFL-CIO-owned Congressmen support this principle and some of them even have the gall to accuse opponents of welfare to strikers of "starving children." It should be pointed out that if one person quits his job for his own reasons and deliberately refuses to work and as a result of his action his children are neglected, then child neglect laws would be quickly enforced. Why should unionists who do the same thing be insulated from prosecution when they break the law?

## VESTED INTERESTS AND STRIKE SUBSIDIES

Numerous attempts have been made at all levels of government to eliminate taxpayer aid to strikers, but year by year the subsidies are becoming more deeply entrenched. The aids take many forms besides unemployment compensation: general-welfare payments, commodities distribution, and food stamps, for example.

Food stamps for strikers have been extensively discussed in Congressional Committee hearings and on the floor of Congress. Farm groups and their high-powered spokesmen in Congress defend particularly the food-stamp and the commodities-distribution programs. Laws usually provide that no food from foreign countries may enter these pipelines—showing that part of the motivation is to raise food prices. On several occasions congressional committees have stated that they would not take sides on strike questions by denying strikers food stamps! In 1970, the House Agriculture Committee refused to put an end to the practice of giving aid to strikers because it "did not wish to take sides in labor disputes."[3] Such reasoning contravenes the Committee's avowed intent to deny participation in the food-stamp program to persons "who are poor because they choose to be poor." But such inconsistency is prevalent in Washington whenever a strike occurs. Bureaucracies in Washington and throughout the land have a vested interest in relief programs, and not only government bureaucracies.

The AFL-CIO has its own vast bureaucracy, which moves quickly

3. *Washington Report,* Chamber of Commerce of USA, Washington, D.C., September-October 1970.

into a strike situation, usually in advance of the strike, and, with trained personnel, helps to set up the local arrangements to get welfare payments started with great dispatch. The Department of Agriculture refuses to furnish data (although it has made unpublished studies) on the extent and scope of food-stamp and commodities distribution to strikers. Undoubtedly, the information is regarded as too hot to handle.

The rising trend of the level and variety of welfare payments and food-stamp handouts in local communities before, during, and after strikes is evidence of the close relationship between the two. The sources mentioned in the footnote on page 141, document this point, as does the *Washington Report* cited above.

The Department of Agriculture, which is in charge of consumer food programs, issued a release dated June 3, 1968, on "Eligibility of Families Without Employment as a Result of Strikes or Labor Difficulties." This stated that the policy is:

> Any family that is determined to be in economic need of food assistance, in accordance with the standards established by a State and approved by the Department of Agriculture, may be certified to receive donated foods. Whether a family is in need of food assistance because of a strike or other labor difficulty has no bearing upon its eligibility to receive food donations.

The food-stamp act of 1964 states, "Refusal to work at a plant or site subject to a strike or a lockout for the duration of such strike or lockout shall not be deemed to be a refusal to accept employment" (Sec. 5(c) ). A provision requiring able-bodied persons to register for work and accept employment elsewhere in order to be eligible for food stamps is apparently ignored when it comes to strikers. Also, in the rush and confusion of expanding the rolls, many are able to fraudulently secure two or more authorizations, as in the case of the teamsters strike in Cook County, Illinois. Verification of asset position is another procedure easily omitted in the haste to begin the program, even though the law may specify that applicants owning assets in excess of some stated figure are ineligible.

When, as frequently happens, union officials help the government relief workers or caseworkers during the rush, nearly everybody on strike is likely to be certified for benefits. Thus, a headline "UAW Speeds Michigan Strikers' Food Stamps" (*Daily World,* October 19, 1970) was followed by the news that during the strike against General Motors, Local 22 of the Cadillac Division had seen to it that most of its more than eight thousand striking members were processed and cleared for the purchase of food stamps.

Clifton Douglas, a Cadillac worker, described the assistance provided by the striking membership to the overburdened welfare staff: "Our members helped by serving coffee and doughnuts, giving out the numbers for interview and providing information to help ease the tension of waiting. The whole program began to function once Local 22 came into the picture."

Strike leaders and union officials have systematically and unabashedly campaigned for public assistance to strikers, through welfare, food-stamp and commodities distribution, and Community Chest or United Fund assistance. The director of the AFL-CIO Community Services Department boasted that during the General Electric strike, such assistance provided as much or more aid to strikers than did union strike benefits. He estimated that the total level of public assistance was $5,000,000 per week. James D. Compton, then chairman of the steering committee, AFL-CIO Coordinated Bargaining Committee, in "Victory at GE: How it Was Done" (*The American Federationist,* July 1970) stated:

> While the [news] papers noted accurately that many strikers had laid aside their own personal strike funds and that strike donations from other workers were of enormous help, they largely overlooked one of the key contributions to the strike's success—that of the AFL-CIO Department of Community Services and its hundreds of local strike committees, which ... showed the way in drawing upon the resources of federal, state and local welfare agencies ... in producing food and financial aid for the strikers and their families.

Yet the case for this favored treatment of one of the contestants in labor disputes is far from clear. Congressman George A. Goodling of Pennsylvania wondered why General Motors should not expect special treatment from the national government to offset strike losses. He told of a worker who paid $18 for food stamps worth $162 at the food stores and commented, "They can't starve us out now that we're getting these food stamps. We can go on forever."

In addition to the network of machinery it has set up to help its member unions and locals, the AFL-CIO provides an endless stream of literature in support of welfare payments to strikers, including rationalizations and arguments formulated for quotation in news conferences and the like. Some of these:

> Taxpayers' dollars are used to feed hungry people abroad.
> Tax dollars are used to feed criminals in prison.
> Tax dollars provide food, shelter, clothing, etc., for enemy prisoners of war.
> Are fellow Americans engaged in industrial warfare entitled to less?
> The criterion for relief should be NEED, whether caused by an act of God, an act of nature, an act of management, or an act of labor.
> It has never been the American tradition to starve those with whom we disagree.

Congressman George Goodling argued for the elimination of food stamps for strikers, citing four points:

> 1) The federal government should not play favorites in a labor-management dispute by granting special privileges to the workers;
> 2) Gainfully employed taxpayers should not be forced to subsidize others who are unemployed by choice;
> 3) The granting of food stamps to strikers can cause prolonged strikes and cause economic damage to the nation and to other workers in related industries who are not on strike; and
> 4) Subsidizing strikers shatters the concept of collective bargaining... collective bargaining becomes "protective bargaining" under this arrangement.

George R. Morris, director of General Motors labor relations, advanced an argument similar to the last one just quoted:

> Strikes serve the function in collective bargaining of bring-
> ing pressure to bear on management and the union to
> reach a settlement. In order to do this, strikes must pinch
> both sides. So public assistance to strikers . . . conflicts
> with the public interest in preserving and strengthening the
> institution of collective bargaining.

Professor Herbert R. Northrup of the University of Pennsylvania,
an authority on labor matters, expressed great concern about strike
subsidies:

> We feel this is becoming a significant welfare cost and is
> having an impact on collective bargaining by making
> strikes longer and settlements higher. From a public-policy
> point of view, we haven't really thought through the
> question of whether we can live with a system where
> strikes don't hurt one party seriously. I don't want any-
> body to starve, but I know collective bargaining can't work
> unless a strike hurts both sides.

Numerous congressmen have polled their constituents on this
question and in every case that has come to my attention, the
citizens, in the quiet of their own homes, have voted decisively
against welfare payments to strikers. Congressman Jackson E. Betts
of Ohio asked, "Should persons who voluntarily strike be entitled to
food stamps?" His constituents who responded voted no in 85.5
percent of the cases. Only 1.3 percent were undecided, an unusually
small proportion on such an issue. In 1972, Congressman Robert H.
Michel of Illinois took numerous steps to induce his colleagues not to
renew food stamps to aid strikers.

Clearly, governments, on a broad front, continue to exacerbate the
massive imbalance in the collective-bargaining scales. Public opinion
is prepared for remedial action, but until legislators put an end to the
raids on welfare and similar funds, they will continue.

There will be more strikes, they will last longer, and the settlements will be more costly to the consumer. Union leaders will find it
more difficult to moderate union demands. Our international balance
of payments will be more unfavorable than it is now and the
pressures for tariff protectionism will grow apace. Indeed, this folly
is weakening the entire social and economic fabric, causing dangerous
domestic and international tensions. Such malaise may become

lethal, while the legislators and key opinion-makers are still searching for a correct diagnosis. If governments continue to aid union officials in maintaining the trend toward overpricing labor, it ill behooves either sector to bemoan persistent unemployment.

Wages and salaries are income, true, but they are also costs—costs immediately to employers, but ultimately to other workers and to consumers generally. If a person knowingly and deliberately starts dosing himself with a lethal poison, he earns little sympathy from his neighbors unless they doubt that he really knoweth not what he doeth.

In the only comprehensive scholarly study of government subsidies for strikers, *Welfare and Strikes: The Use of Public Funds to Support Strikers* the authors conclude:

> . . . paying welfare benefits to strikers is an unwarranted imposition on the public treasury and the private good. Organized labor's relative bargaining power before public support was certainly great enough to be influential. The additional power which $329 million in direct benefits can buy may well upset the relative bargaining positions of unions and management so greatly that the fundamental structure of collective bargaining will be seriously threatened. The general public must pay the costs, not only directly through higher taxes and higher prices, but also indirectly through greater disruption to the economic system and through inflation.[4]

In spite of these conclusions the raids on the public purse go on. In Michigan in the summer of 1972 employees of the Dow Chemical Company went on strike; by earning as little as $1 to $18 elsewhere at temporary employment, they qualified for unemployment compensation, charged for the most part against the Dow Chemical Company! Government, deeply concerned with the cost-push and legislating direct controls, nevertheless keeps on building up the economic power of the union officials and the unions and therefore also indirectly the power of nonmembers.

---

4. Armand J. Thieblot, Jr., and Ronald M. Cowin, *Welfare and Strikes: The Use of Public Funds to Support Strikers* (Philadelphia, Pa.: University of Pennsylvania Press, 1972), p. 276. Dr. Northrup provided a foreword. A review of this book, plus additional current information, appeared in *Human Events*, July 1, 1972, p. 4.

# MINIMUM WAGE RIGIDITIES

Careful economic studies have demonstrated that minimum wage laws tend to increase unemployment, particularly among teenagers, the unskilled, and minority groups. Because a rise in the minimum wage has a ratchet effect on wage scales above the minimum, wage costs generally are raised and tend to induce unemployment and enhance international balance-of-payments difficulties. Economists, including many liberals, have advised against further minimum wage increases. However, union officials, even those whose members are paid far above the minimum, uniformly favor higher minima; there must be an explanation beyond pure altruism.

One effect of a universal minimum wage would be to deny private employment to all workers not producing work worth the legal minimum. A worker who produced a net value of $1.60 an hour for an employer could not be expected to hold on to a job very long if he had to be paid $2.00 an hour. Employers, either by careful inspection, or by scientific studies of jobs, tasks, and outputs, can determine with considerable accuracy the number and the ability of workers worth keeping on the payroll.

Those denied private employment would be the neediest—the elderly, the physically handicapped, the very young, the teenagers lacking training and work experience. Only public institutions could afford to employ those thus unemployed. Nonetheless, in this country, as well as in most Western countries, a universal minimum wage is popularly regarded as an act of social justice and a part of the "war on poverty." Failing the provision of public jobs paying at least

143

as much as the displaced workers could have earned in the competitive labor market, these objects of our concern would have to depend on relatives, friends or neighbors, or on private or public charity.

The higher the minimum, the larger will be the number of able and willing workers forced into idleness, an idleness many of them would resent as humiliating. Some few would become self-employed independent entrepreneurs, such as abound in the crowded cities of the poorer countries, the ubiquitous shoeshine boys, the peddlers who buy wholesale and sell door-to-door, or on public streets, products of dubious quality. A minimum wage can never reach the self-employed, but it can force many who lack the capital, the inclination, and the qualifications for entrepreneurship to take on the risk. They will maintain their self-respect at great personal cost, and society as a whole is poorly served.

The effects of a *partial* minimum wage are different, and the differences should be noted, because the laws now in effect cover only a part of the labor force. They do not set a universal minimum wage; they apply to specific employers, those falling in particular categories, who may not hire workers for wages less than those specified in the relevant laws. Other employers may hire on terms set by competitive market forces. In the short run, the latter may actually benefit from a newly imposed minimum wage law, because workers denied employment in the covered fields will force down wages in the uncovered fields. Partial minimum wage laws will almost certainly cause some transitional unemployment but *need not* cause any long-term unemployment.

There is no reason why the wage component in the gross national product (GNP) should be affected, though the inequalities in labor's share would be increased—those working within the covered fields getting somewhat more, those working in competitive fields getting somewhat less. The composition of the GNP would be affected, consisting of more goods and services produced by firms in the competitive fields and less by those in the protected fields. The GNP would be smaller as a result of the misallocation of resources and all of us as consumers would be worse off. But the chief victims would not be the profit makers, the receivers of interest and rents, but the workers in the competitive fields. Workers would compete against workers. Minimum wage laws reduce fair and open-market competition in the labor market.

The increased competition from firms in the uncovered fields makes it more difficult for unions operating in those areas to secure wages comparable to those secured by unions bargaining with firms that are covered by minimum wage laws. This is particularly true if those administering the laws take "minimum" to mean the wages determined by collective bargaining, rather than those provided by the laws themselves often in vaguely worded definitions. The state, not the union, enforces such contracts. Consequently, unions operating in the competitive fields are apt to discover that violence or the threat of violence is a necessary part of the bargaining process. Furthermore, their spokesmen become reconciled to something organized labor has traditionally opposed—the enactment of a *universal* minimum wage. The relevance of this will become clear presently.

## THE 1930s MINIMUM WAGE LAWS

The slack markets of the 1930s induced state governments to expand minimum wage laws, and forced the national government to enter this field with a flood of labor market interventions. In March 1931, Congress adopted, and President Hoover signed into law, the Davis-Bacon Act. The secretary of labor was required to determine the "prevailing wages" acceptable for bids on federal projects. In effect, it set a minimum wage for federally financed construction work. This was a dramatic reversal of the previous policy of awarding government contracts at the lowest cost to the taxpayer.

In 1935, Congress adopted, and President Roosevelt signed into law, the Walsh-Healey Act, which applied a closely similar wage test to federal-government-purchase contracts of $10,000 or more. As defined in the act, the wage was to be: "The prevailing minimum wage for persons employed in similar work or in the particular or similar industries or groups of industries currently operating *in the locality* in which the material, supplies, articles or equipment are to be manufactured or finished under its contract." Again, the policy of low-cost procurement was abandoned. This law did not fix any definite minimum wage rate, but, as federal spending increased in practice, it had a powerful wage-raising impact, as did the Davis-Bacon Act.

In 1933, the National Industrial Recovery Act (NIRA) provided for fixed minimum wages under the industry codes. The Guffey Coal Act of 1935 did the same for the coal industry. Similar laws provided for minimum wage fixing in the Merchant Marine in 1936 and in sugar processing in 1937. In 1935 the NIRA and the Guffey Coal Act were declared unconstitutional by the U. S. Supreme Court. In 1938 Congress adopted a broad wage-and-hour law covering interstate commerce. This Fair Labor Standards Act provided for an increase in minimum wage rates over several years, and a 50-percent labor-cost penalty on hours in excess of forty-four, then forty-two, and finally forty, after two years.

The outlawing of the NIRA and the Guffey Coal Act won spokesmen for organized labor over to the need for a universal minimum wage. Unfortunately, from their point of view, the Constitution and the political realities prevented the enactment of anything approaching a universal nationwide minimum. The Supreme Court had held that the Congress lacked the power to fix wages in general. The temper of the times made it clear, however, that the Court would uphold a law that affected only those employers engaged in interstate commerce, provided a suitable justification could be incorporated into the law. So, in 1938, the Congress duly passed the Fair Labor Standards Act with "findings in fact," which the Court specifically referred to as the basis for its finding that the Act constituted a valid exercise of the commerce clause. The findings declared that low wages and long hours adversely affect the health, efficiency, and general well-being of employees, constitute unfair methods of competition, and cause labor disputes, strikes, and interference with the orderly and fair marketing of goods in interstate commerce.

The act might never have been passed had the adjective "fair" not been attached to the title and had its supporters not accepted "escape clauses" that in effect exempted the vast majority of employers—those in agriculture (whose products certainly moved in interstate commerce) and the host of small businesses that were little or not at all involved in interstate commerce. Thus the law that we shall be concerned with in this chapter, like the Davis-Bacon and the Walsh-Healey Acts, is a partial minimum wage law, wider in scope than the other two and resting on a different constitutional basis, but nonetheless partial.

## MISTAKEN APPROACH TO WAGE IMPROVEMENT

Clearly, much of the public and most politicians had abounding faith in the government's ability to improve conditions by setting aside market forces. The Great Depression had been a period of underused resources: office space, apartments and other housing, retailing space, industrial plants, raw materials, *and labor.* All prices fell. The Congress, however, provided a minimum price only for labor, thus barring workers from a host of industries and jobs unless they could find employers willing and able to pay the various minima required by the different laws and by their administrators. The length and depth of the Depression were due in part to wage rigidities resulting from these laws, though in greater part to the failure of the monetary policy.

The Federal Reserve Board (FED) had allowed the money supply to shrink by more than one-third from August 1929, to March 1933, in line with the accepted economic opinion at that time, without realizing that its policies were forcing up the value of the dollar (forcing down prices in general), and causing businesses and individuals to defer investing and spending until prices showed some evidence of having reached a bottom. Through mis-diagnosis and ignorance, government became, in effect, the underwriter of the longest and most severe depression in our history. The economic system had not broken down; through ignorance, the monetary authorities had failed to play the role that virtually all students now recognize as the proper one for a central bank. This breakdown was discussed in Chapter VI, but a brief review is needed here.

The plethora of minimum wage laws barred many workers from employment. The Wagner Act, passed in 1935 to replace the NIRA codes, put the central government into the position of supporting unionism and the drives for higher wage costs. But when World War II broke out, we still had some 10,000,000 workers unemployed.[1] Not surprisingly, the government medicine of the 1930s did not cure. The New Deal failed because it failed to restore spending and investing incentives. A price increase generally reduces purchases. It would be strange indeed if a rise in the minimum wage did not increase unemployment.

## HIGHER MINIMUM IMPACT ON TOTAL WAGE STRUCTURE

Another result of a rise in the minimum wage is that it also tends to raise wages that are above the minimum; customary or historic wage differentials are highly prized by employees. Obviously, if workers who are paid just above the previous minimum rate now have their wages overtaken by a rise in the minimum, the employer, in good conscience, must raise the wages of those near the minimum; but this internal wage stress may apply far up the line, affecting all wage rates within a plant, trade, or industry.

Thus a rise in the minimum wage makes all or most labor more expensive, and the employer is always under competitive pressure to minimize the use of overpriced factors of production. Even a monopolist evades the cost-price push when he can. Union officials, aware of the upward pressures of a higher minimum wage scale on the wage structure generally, are its most vocal advocates, but they disregard the inevitable disemployment impact among all grades of labor, not just the minimum grade.

## ECONOMIC STUDIES OF MINIMUM WAGE LAWS

Since numerous factors affect employment, layoffs, and reemployment, as well as compensation, it is not easy to pinpoint the disem-

---

1. The most thorough analysis of the mistaken diagnosis of our depression troubles is found in *The Great Contraction 1929-1933*, by Milton Friedman and Anna Schwartz (New York, N.Y.: National Bureau of Economic Reasearch, 1965).

ployment impact of a rise in the minimum wage. Union officials argue that there is no evidence that increased minimum wages have led to unemployment. Government reports generally advance the same argument. If this is so, why not raise the minimum another dollar or two per hour?

Plenty of scholars with no axes to grind reject this agnosticism. Professors John M. Peterson and Charles T. Stewart, for example, found convincing evidence to support the view that statutory wage minimums have adverse employment effects.[2] They found that higher minimum wage rates had slowed employment growth more in low-wage industries in the South than in the same industries in high-wage areas less affected by the increase. The lowest-wage plants experienced the most adverse employment effects. In Puerto Rico, minimum wages caused a large and measurable loss of manufacturing employment and an immeasurable, but undoubtedly still greater, potential loss.

Summing up, Peterson and Stewart concluded that the "impression created in most government studies that federal minimum wage policy has produced no adverse employment effects is erroneous." In fact, the regressive distribution of these effects—gains for some workers at the expense of others who are less well off—invalidates the unqualified claim that statutory wage minimums help the poor, and "brings into question both the wisdom and equity of such minimums."

Dr. Yale Brozen of the University of Chicago has published a long list of studies demonstrating similar conclusions.[3] Dr. Arthur F. Burns has measured the impact of increases in the legal minimum wage and found the disemployment effect clear and distinct. Since World War II particularly, he noted, employers have found ways to replace many unskilled and semiskilled laborers with machines and automated equipment manned by a few skilled operators. As a result, unskilled wages relative to skilled wages should have dropped; instead

---

2. *Employment Effects of Minimum Wage Rates* (Washington, D.C.: American Enterprise Institute, 1969).

3. See, for example, "The Effect of Statutory Minimum Wage Increases on Teenage Employment," *Journal of Law and Economics.* Chicago, Ill., April 1969.

they increased year after year, making it increasingly difficult for unskilled workers to find jobs at a time when large numbers of inexperienced women and teenagers were seeking employment. The central government helped powerfully, after 1949, to induce a strong "upward drift across the years in the actual ratio of the minimum wage to the average wage."[4]

*During the postwar years, Dr. Burns states, the ratio of the unemployment rate of teenagers to that of male adults was invariably higher during the six months following the increase of the minimum wage than it was in the preceding half year. The ratio of the unemployment rate of female adults to that of male adults has behaved similarly.* Furthermore, the rise in unemployment among nonwhite teenagers greatly exceeded the rise among white teenagers. As Friedman has noted, "Insofar as minimum wage laws have any effect at all, this effect is clearly to increase poverty," and he referred to the wage-and-hour law of 1938 as "the most anti-Negro law on our statute books—in its effect, not its intent."

## REGIONAL DISTORTIONS OF UNIFORM MINIMUM WAGES

A uniform nationwide minimum wage law, in a nation in which differences in the human and natural resources vary widely from region to region and from community to community within regions, is bound to have a more adverse impact on employment in the areas where the marginal productivity of labor is lowest. These areas become still less attractive as locations for all the firms that are subject to the law. "The mobility of capital is reduced. An unnecessarily large out-movement of population from low-wage and low-levels-of-living areas must occur if the sound principle of equal real pay for comparable work is to be realized."[5]

The minimum wage laws, like uniform nationwide collectively

---

4. *The Management of Prosperity* (New York, N.Y.: Columbia University Press, 1965).

5. Quoted from *Introduction to Economics* (New York, N.Y.: Van Nostrand, 1954), p. 461. op. cit.

bargained wage rates, protect the firms situated in more developed areas against firms in the poorer and less-developed areas. They reduce the ability of the latter to attract the capital and enterprise needed to make workers more productive in these areas, where they may happen to have been born and raised and to which they may have become deeply attached. They protect higher paid workers against lower paid workers. Instead of allowing capital to remain more mobile than labor, such laws require workers to be more mobile than is economically and socially desirable. They stimulated the vast migration of relatively unskilled whites and blacks from the South to the North after World War II and of Puerto Ricans from their lovely island to the ghettos of northern cities, to the detriment of tranquility, and law and order.

As early as 1937 Walter Lippmann in *The Good Society* had warned against efforts to uproot people in massive fashion from their moorings and to transfer them to a new and different type of environment. He said, ". . . tides of population must move slowly if old communities are not to be devitalized by emigration and new communities overwhelmed by unassimilable immigration." Dr. Van Sickle notes that the New Deal, in its plan to ameliorate the well-being of people in the Old South, opted for encouraging migration out of the South instead of encouraging the flow of investment job-making capital into that region. The NIRA and most other minimum wage statutes encouraged nationwide uniform minima, and thereby damaged the prospects of the regions and areas where the productivity of labor was low. Millions of sincere people in the North supported these measures, but as Van Sickle noted, "The *interested* supporters of the Fair Labor Standards Act (Wage and Hour law of 1938, and its amendments) wanted a law that would reduce, not increase, the severity of the competition coming up from the South, as is very apparent from arguments presented in its defense as set forth in the Congressional Record."[6]

Alchian and Allen in *University Economics* (previously cited) put the same idea in these words:

---

6. John V. Van Sickle, *Freedom in Jeopardy; The Tyranny of Idealism* (New York, N.Y.: The World Publishing Company, 1969), p. 105.

If Southern and Puerto Rican labor have to be paid a higher wage, they cannot compete so effectively against Northern laborers. It should come as no surprise to learn that the United States Congress's support for minimum wage laws comes primarily from Northern Congressmen, who profess to be trying to help the poorer Southern laborers. (Page 487.)

Dr. James Tobin of Yale is generally regarded as a liberal; after he left the President's Council of Economic Advisers (in the Kennedy Administration) he stated:

... people who lack the capacity to earn a decent living ... will not be helped by minimum wage laws, trade union pressures or other devices which seek to compel employers to pay them more than they are worth.

Dr. Paul Samuelson, certainly no conservative, remarked, "What good does it do a black youth to know that an employer must pay him $1.60 per hour if the fact that he must be paid that amount is what keeps him from getting a job?"

More than a quarter of a century ago, Dr. George Stigler of the University of Chicago said that if there is anything on which economists ought to agree it is that a minimum wage law will not rescue the most poor from their poverty. Actually, there is now widespread agreement on that point.

Economists are not the only ones aware of the damaging impact of minimum wage fixing. A. Philip Randolph, former president of the Brotherhood of Sleeping Car Porters, reported in March 1967 to the AFL-CIO executive council, meeting in Florida, that Negro and other agricultural workers were being disemployed in some areas as a result of the changes in the wage-and-hour law. Mitchell I. Ginsberg, Administrator of New York City Human Resources Administration, has urged government subsidizing of jobs. He said, "If a man is worth only 60 percent of the going wage during his training period, the employer would be permitted to pay this and the government would provide the other 40 percent. In this way we make sure he gets training that will keep him from being a welfare case."[7]

---

7. *The New York Times,* October 2, 1968.

Dr. Daniel P. Moynihan, who has devoted most of his adult life to efforts to improve the lot of the poor, had this to say in congressional hearings on urban affairs on December 13, 1966:

> It doesn't make any sense for us to continue to escalate the level of the minimum wage ... in order to try to produce a family income—at the same time that minimum wage seems to be ominously close to raising the level of unemployment.
>
> For example, last week in New York City, the Director of the Bureau of Labor Statistics in that city, Mr. Bienstock, reported that in the metropolitan areas he was surveying, 41 percent of the teenagers in the work force were unemployed. Now if 41 percent are unemployed at $1.25 an hour wage—what will happen with a $2 minimum wage?

## MISALLOCATION OF RESOURCES

The Davis-Bacon and Walsh-Healey Acts have also had disallocative effects, in part similar to, and in part different from those of the wage-and-hour law.

*The Walsh-Healey Act.* This act has had internal protectionist effects similar to those produced by the minimum wage law. Thus, in *The Walsh-Healey Public Contracts Act,* Dr. Van Sickle noted that in fiscal year 1950 the firms in the eleven states of the Southeast received only 7.25 percent of the Walsh-Healey contracts by number, and 4.6 percent by value, despite the fact that 21 percent of our total population resided in these states, and that the firms situated there were responsible for 13 percent of total wages and salaries earned in 1950.[8]

An examination of the same law led Herbert C. Morton of the Brookings Institution in 1965 to recommend its repeal. Carrol L. Christenson and Richard A. Myren came to the same conclusion in their *Wage Policy under the Walsh-Healey Public Contracts Act.* They demonstrated that the law, and more particularly its administration

---

8. See Van Sickle's *Freedom in Jeopardy,* op. cit.

(due to its dubious interpretation of the locally prevailing wage doctrine), had enabled the unions recognized by firms working on government contracts to make inordinate gains, thus exerting a powerful upward thrust on already high wage rates.

*The Davis-Bacon Act.* This act requires that workers employed on every contract in excess of $2,000, to which the United States or the District of Columbia is a party, for construction, alterations, including painting and decorating, or repair of public buildings or public works shall be paid no less than the rates determined by the Secretary of Labor *to be prevailing on similar projects in the area* in which the work is to be performed.

These provisions have been extended or amended to apply to no less than fifty-seven federal government programs and activities—the Federal Civil Defense Act of 1950, the Federal-Aid Highway Act of 1956, the Mental Retardation Facilities Construction Act, the Library Services and Construction Act, etc. Some thirty-five states have similar laws on their books. The burden placed on the Secretary of Labor and other officials by the requirement that they find the *local prevailing* wage for thousands of contracts covering all the different occupational skills in the building trades boggles the mind, but this provides lucrative jobs for bureaucrats and labor-union officials and employees. Meantime, the excluded workers, not covered by the minimum wage act, pay in lower wages, and all of us in higher taxes. But there is much worse.[9]

Laws coming from Congress are rarely unambiguous or obvious, particularly as soon as a law has to be applied to specific cases. Interpretive regulations, while necessary, can easily be abused. One section of the regulations of the Davis-Bacon Act has opened vast opportunities for wage raising. This law does not fix a minimum wage; it is intended only to prevent local labor from being underbid by lower-paid nonlocal labor brought into the locality by outside

---

9. Some scholarly research has begun only recently to expose the inappropriate, possibly illegal and fraudulent interpretation and application in the administration of Davis-Bacon cases. See particularly John P. Gould, *Davis-Bacon Act: The Economics of Prevailing Wage Laws* (Washington, D.C.: American Enterprise Institute, 1971). Most of the information here was obtained from that study.

contractors. The purpose of Congress was quite clear and obvious. But Section 1.6(b) of the regulations provides that if no similar construction had occurred within the last year, the authorities can set wage rates paid on "the *nearest* similar construction." (Italics supplied.)

The General Accounting Office of the United States government (GAO) has uncovered widespread disregard for the law and the regulations. Wage determinations for power-equipment operators on federally financed projects throughout Maine were found to be based on the much higher union-negotiated rates in far off Boston, Massachusetts! Workers employed concurrently on both private and federal projects received wages on the federal projects that were from 68 to 221 percent higher than those on the private projects. The GAO found that the Davis-Bacon bureau people included previous Davis-Bacon rates in the information used to determine "prevailing" wages for new projects—thereby carrying forward earlier errors. So far, no one has gone to prison or paid any fines or refunds for these blatant violations of the law and its purposes.

In a housing project for the Marine Corps School at Quantico, Virginia, the Labor Department wage-rate determinations were from 28 to 100 percent higher than those found by the Navy's own wage-rate survey. The Labor Department admitted its error, and issued a new determination with lower rates. Within a month, however, in response to union protests, the Labor Department knuckled under and reissued the *original* wage rates. Again there were no penalties.

Dr. Gould summarizes the findings of Professor Damodar M. Gujarati (from his article in *Journal of Business,* University of Chicago, July 1967) covering a careful analysis of 372 Department of Labor Davis-Bacon determinations. The results were shocking. For example, he found that in many cases union wage rates were "imported" into a locality from noncontiguous counties or from statewide wage data. The law defined the area of construction as the "city, town, village, or other civil subdivision of the state in which the work is performed." This definition was intended to prevent "leap-frogging," i.e., to protect *local* wage rates, not to raise them by determinations based on rates from distant higher-paying areas. From 25 to more than 50 percent of the determinations were based on rates in noncontiguous territory, sometimes from clear out of the state.

In 1970, Dr. Arthur F. Burns urged the suspension or repeal of the Davis-Bacon Act, and the president suspended the law on February 23, 1971. But the suspension lasted hardly more than a month, to March 29. The *quid pro quo*, according to Dr. Gould, was an agreement to a program of "voluntary" wage restraint that was to keep negotiated wages to an annual increase of about 6 percent. The reaction of the union, Dr. Gould says, "is interesting because it is a piece of evidence which strongly substantiates many of the findings of this survey. It appears that the unions were willing to accept the quasi-regulated wage constraints, which they had previously rejected, in return for the reinstatement of the Davis-Bacon Act." Davis-Bacon, as administered by the Labor Department, was the better bargain!

## SUMMARY

Minimum wage laws, originally conceived as instruments to improve the lot of the poor, are increasingly being recognized for what they are—measures that price the poorest out of the labor market. Records show a rise in the unemployment of the unskilled, and untrained, the youngsters and, particularly, the nonwhite teenagers.

Minimum wage laws create wage rigidity and make the economy less flexible. They penalize capital-poor areas and the workers living in those areas. Union leaders strongly support these laws, and press for continuous increases in the minima, recognizing that each increase helps push up much of the entire wage structure, not just the minimum wage.

The laws have proved highly inflationary. With wages constituting some 75 percent of all costs, final prices had to be allowed to rise if unemployment was to be kept at a politically acceptable level; and this despite the damage the rise was doing to our balance-of-payments position. The August 1971 decision to suspend payments in gold to our foreign creditors was due in no small part to the way in which these laws had strengthened the wage-push on the American economy. Burns undoubtedly had this in mind when, in his testimony before the House Banking and Currency Committee (March 2, 1972), he emphasized the need for restraint:

> To assure success in these objectives of foreign economic policy, we must have skillful and fully responsible management of monetary and fiscal affairs. The objectives of our foreign economic policy and of our domestic economic policy are interdependent. For the sake of both the one and the other we will need to concentrate on stepping up sharply the productivity of our resources and on regaining prosperity without inflation.

Minimum wage laws make no contribution to reaching this urgent target. Indeed, they are on the side of inflation, rising-wage costs, and the misallocation of resources.

157

# CAN COLLECTIVE BARGAINING ADVANCE JUSTICE AND EQUITY?

Union officials and union literature (articles, pamphlets, resolutions, etc.) always reiterate that the union goal is a fair day's pay for a fair day's work. Justice and equity, they say, are what they seek in dealing with employers. But these terms—fairness, justice, equity—are not objectively definable. No one, of course, favors unfair, unjust, or inequitable wages or working conditions. How useful, then, is the question raised by the title of this chapter?

Since union leaders describe their goals in these terms, the concepts should be discussed, despite their vagueness. Not that the problem of concreteness is confined to labor questions. The "Rule of Law," and "a government of laws and not of men," are common expressions, even though many pages would be needed to spell out their meaning and their essentiality in our society. "Due process" is not a self-explanatory phrase, yet no one but an anarchist or a dictator would deny its key importance to a decent and orderly society.

## SECTIONAL BARGAINING

Collective bargaining is sectional bargaining. Specific settlements are not made for labor as a whole, or even for unionized labor as a whole. Collective bargaining is carried on for an individual local union, or for a metropolitan, regional, or nationwide group in a given trade, or occupation, or industry.

Professor Thomas Sowell of UCLA, questioned whether unions have aided labor as a whole, replied:

> Through unionization, specific union leaders gained greatly, and members of some unions acquired important differential advantages which could be maintained only by excluding other workers from employment opportunities—these other workers being typically from further down the social-economic scale, often black. . . . Of course, workers are much better off today, when the whole national income is higher, than they were in the past, but the same is true of many groups, organized and unorganized. Those who deal in symbolism rather than substance can still claim that Labor has improved its relative position, meaning by Labor the organized minority of workers who were better off even before unionization. Those who had have gotten more. . . .[1]

A former airline pilot, George E. Hopkins, revealed in the frank title of his book, *The Airline Pilots: A Study in Elite Unionization,* the preferential gains of the Air Line Pilots Association (ALPA).[2] Salaries of over $60,000 per year for a three-day week place pilots at the apex of employees. The author frankly attributes the high remuneration to the "hard-hitting collective bargaining of ALPA," and not to pilot supply and demand, or public requirements and demands for air travel, or such factors as skills, responsibilities, and risks. If so, what of equity and fairness?

Actually, any union's literature and oratory are replete with self-congratulatory accounts of how it has outpaced the other unions, the others often being named and identified. A generation or so ago, railroad workers were at or near the top of the economic ladder among all unionized trades; their descent down the ladder has been the cause of much anguish and criticism—of their officials, their employers, and the ICC. Their massive wage settlements since the mid-1960s were wangled in spite of the insolvency of many of the

---

1. "Violence and the Pay-Off Society," *University of Chicago Magazine,* November-December 1971.

2. Cambridge, Mass., Harvard University Press, 1971. See *Wall Street Journal* for a short review by Mary Peterson, January 21, 1972, editorial page.

railroads. "Equity" dictated that they regain their former relative superiority in the union hierarchy.

Indeed, when I first started to study economic history and the history of the labor movement, I made what I thought was a major discovery: that the lowest-paid workers rarely made any demands; that labor unrest, strikes and higher-wage demands invariably came not from the lower economic strata, but from the most affluent working groups or trades within the economy. This was a somewhat disturbing discovery, because I had been led to believe that the union movement was primarily concerned with equity, and particularly with the poverty of the lowest-paid workers.

Unions are almost exclusively concerned with maximizing economic gains for their members, or rather for those who can hold or get jobs on the new and higher terms. The adverse impact on other workers is ignored. As Samuel Gompers frankly admitted, the goal of every union is "more." Does this make the goal fair, equitable, and just? Only if, as union spokesmen claim, "a rise in wages anywhere raises wages everywhere," a comforting but obviously impossible phenomenon.

According to union lore, a strike is called against an employer. This is at best a partial truth. Authenticated reports on union violence during strikes disclose that unions operate against other workers. In the 1971-72 strike against the Richmond, Virginia, newspapers scores of acts of violence occurred against employees, with no violence against the person or the plant of the employer. The union's fundamental purpose (Chapter II) was to take its members out of competition.

The competition that thus concerns the union is often between workers—for a particular job or line of work—not between the workers on the one hand and the employer on the other. To increase its members' pay and other emoluments a union may aim to reduce the supply of labor available to a specific employer. This means the exclusion of other workers.

Unions employ a variety of devices to this end. The closed union, closed shop, union shop, apprentice limitations, and, in professional circles, licensure requirements with stiff examinations and tests—all these reduce the labor supply in a given trade, occupation, or profession. Clearly, what is sought is not equity or fairness but the betterment of the position of one group of workers at the expense of another group. The result is that many workers are marginal, or submarginal, who would not otherwise have been.[3] This makes a farce of union talk about fair, equitable and just remuneration.

No one who gave the matter careful thought would expect bargaining that is carried out on thousands of separate fronts, via a myriad of local, regional, national, and international conferences to yield a "just" or "fair" wage pattern across the land. A, for example, may be a very weak union, B a most powerful one. Between these antipodes there are almost infinite degrees of power. It would be a miracle if such disparities in bargaining strength produced even a semblance of consistent justice or equity.

Peter Wiles, an English scholar and economist, in an article entitled "Are Trade Unions Necessary?" put the matter this way:

> It is truly amazing that anyone should suppose this crude, selfish, violent and piecemeal process to contribute to social justice. It is, when we come to think of it, incredible that the building up by some salary and wage earners of monopoly power, in greater degree here and lesser degree there, should improve the distribution of income among them all; so incredible that the supposition has only to be directly given utterance to be dismissed.[4]

Union tactics vary. Some oppose violence, and even tough talk. Others rely on the strike, on the use of violence, on the building up of envy and antagonism toward the employer, and on exploiting all the baser human traits. Strike funds are called war chests. Some unions build up good relations and good will at the place of employment; others do the opposite. But, regardless of tactics, in the final analysis the strength of unionism depends on the popular but mistaken belief that unions promote social justice, that violence is all right when it is the only way to prevent capital from exploiting labor.

---

3. Clarence B. Carson, *The War on the Poor* (New Rochelle, N.Y.: Arlington House, 1969). Chapter V of this volume shows how government unites with union officials to make war on the poor.

4. Quoted from *Encounter* with permission. London, September 1956.

The general public does not know how effectively competition protects wage-takers from wage-givers—all of them, and not just a privileged minority. Steel companies, for example, face competition not only from one another and from foreign sources, but from other materials. The American automobile industry is highly concentrated (the four largest companies do more than 80 percent of the business), but the competition between the four is fierce. They encounter strong competition from abroad, and also from used cars, which are always a part of the total automobile supply. The whole industry competes with railroads, buses, and airplanes as alternative modes of travel.

An employer facing vigorous competition in his own line, or from substitutes, may take a strike before acceding to uneconomic union demands. Consequently, union officials usually strike a stronger employer, and then insist that the weaker ones surrender and make the same settlement. Wherever possible, union officials try to sweep all employers in any given line into a single net (say, department stores, restaurants, or construction companies) so that all employers in the line are forced to meet the same surrender terms. But, even so, unionized clerks in department stores, for example, may earn $2 an hour, while truck drivers, newspaper mail clerks, or garbage workers are paid at three to five times that rate. Clearly, unions do not bring about justice or equity, even among unionists.

Most publicized wage increases arouse the envy of workers in other unions. Correcting the resulting "inequities" invariably creates new inequities. So it goes, round and round—something that could not occur in an open market where adjustments proceed silently, smoothly, constantly, and without fanfare or publicity.


## "ABILITY TO PAY" AND EQUITY

In pressing his demands, the union official selects his key arguments with care. Against an employer who has enjoyed good profits for a year or two, he advances the ability-to-pay argument; against one in financial difficulties, he dusts off the equal-pay-for-equal-work argument. The first is particularly popular, despite the fact that if wage differentials were based on profit differentials, a weird and utterly unethical pattern of wages would result. Companies taking losses would pay very low wages; the most profitable would pay the highest, with a bewildering range in between. Workers with equal skills in the same trade, in the same industry in a community might earn wildly varied wage rates. If wages are to be based on productivity, it is the productivity of *the economy as a whole* that should largely govern wage rates and wage changes, with enough variations to accommodate expanding and contracting enterprises.

In a reasonably competitive free-market economy, wage changes would distribute a major share of the annual GNP increases to all claimants in the form of slowly declining consumer prices, and, in addition, would steadily reallocate resources in response to consumer demands.

Peter Wiles (in the article cited earlier) argued that the gains of technical progress should be passed on to the consumer. He showed succinctly the evils of basing wage and salary changes on the variations in technical progress, industry by industry:

> Thus since the Middle Ages there has been great technical progress in the production of wheat, a little in the building of houses, and none in the saving of souls. Yet the relative incomes of farmers, bricklayers and priests have not, after making all qualifications, greatly changed; nor should they have. Bricklayer and priest both benefit from the new relative cheapness of bread. Had the economy been properly unionized all this time, the farmers would have collared all that benefit, and priests would still be on a medieval standard of living (p. 9).

I. W. Abel, president of the Steelworkers Union and a member of the wage-control Pay Board from late 1971 to early 1972 lashed out at the massive wage settlements granted to the construction trades under a separate government-control system called "Construction Industry Stabilization Committee" with Professor John Dunlop as chairman. Abel promptly got news-media kudos for what was thought to be a spirit of moderation. Noticing this mistake, Abel publicly denied any intention of curbing the size of construction wage increases.[5] He merely demanded that his steelworkers not be short-changed in the deal.

Few writers have pointed out more clearly than Frederic Bastiat (1801-1850) the way in which legalized power, whether in the hands of the state or of private groups, threatens personal liberty and individual dignity. In his most famous book, *The Law*, Bastiat described socialism and communism, under whatever labels they might appear, as forms of legalized plunder. In *Frederic Bastiat: A Man Alone*, Dr. George C. Roche summarizes Bastiat's position:

> Recognizing that the law is organized force, Bastiat made it clear that such legal plunder could only be *legalized injustice*. He went on to emphasize that such organized injustice finally proves so corrupting to the fabric of society as to destroy all social progress, and ultimately, all individual development.[6]

Bastiat was concerned both with plunder by governments and plunder by private persons and groups permitted by government. He said: "We recognize the right of every man to perform services for himself or to serve others according to conditions arrived at through free bargaining." By this he meant truly *free*, uncoerced bargaining. He put it this way:

> Try to imagine a system of labor imposed by force that is not a violation of liberty; a transfer of wealth imposed by force that is not a violation of property rights. If you cannot do so, then you must agree that the law cannot organize labor and industry without organized injustice.

The more human relations, economic activity, production, and trade rest on free, willing decisions and willing exchanges, the greater the prospects of social harmony. It will not produce a Utopia, but it will maximize harmony, justice, and equity more nearly than any dictator ever could.

It is easy to assume that government can assure fair shares for all and improve the distribution of the national output. Perhaps it can.

---

5. *Business Week,* March 11, 1972, pp. 108-09.
6. New Rochelle, N.Y., Arlington House, 1971.

But if so, it will be through its taxing and spending powers and not through collective bargaining. And there is no evidence that government action or government fiat leads to fairer distribution of output. What generally happens is that the government helps the not-so-poor at the expense of the poor. It makes war on the really poor. Government welfare programs usually and rather quickly get transformed into plundering raids directed against the general taxpayers and particularly against the very poor.[7]

The senior senator from one of the New England states in a speech in 1970 to a labor-union convention said, "You should have an employer like we senators have: we fix our own salaries." Such pandering to callous greed fosters the worst in man—not the best.

In answering the question posed in the title of his article, ("Are Trade Unions Necessary?") Peter Wiles said ". . . in strict economics there is scarcely any case for the continued existence of trade unions in a fully employed welfare state." And indeed it is hard to see how in such an economy the labor union could perform any constructive *economic* function.

Some may regard the question as sheer heresy. But changing conditions tend to make old institutions obsolete, even destructive of human values. Thus Adam Smith nearly two hundred years ago dared question the extreme trade protectionism of his day, and, in questioning it, contributed to its downfall. He showed how saving and investing and "the unseen hand" of competition created widespread social and economic benefits that were not part of the intentions of those who did the saving and investing, and carried on productive enterprises. Smith wrote at a time when trade protectionism enjoyed even greater respect than trade unionism does today. Trade unionism, as it presently operates in the United States, has made workers as a whole poorer than they would otherwise have been. It should by now be clear that revocation of the present immunities and ex-

---

7. A reading of Dr. Clarence B. Carson, op cit., will quickly disabuse any objective-minded person of the idea that government fosters equity and justice. If the Goddess of Justice is blind, as we are told she is, we will get more equity and justice through the play of impersonal market forces than through the play of political forces. For further development of this point see also *Freedom in Jeopardy* by John V. Van Sickle, op. cit.

emptions extended to unions would make it unnecessary to abolish them.

Merryle S. Rukeyser in *Collective Bargaining: The Power to Destroy* examined the undue power of the labor union and concluded that some legislative changes and a greater sense of responsibility on the part of union officials and members would make more drastic action unnecessary.[8]

A Brookings Institution report, in a series entitled *Studies of Unionism in Government,* although concerned primarily with the administration of wages, salaries, etc. and day-to-day personnel affairs, addressed itself also to the question of the fairness and equity of union-negotiated contracts. On that question, the report is confusing and somewhat contradictory, yet it states, "Although job evaluation factors, personnel shortages, and prevailing rates are earnestly discussed in the bargaining process, they are less important to the final decision than is the sheer political power of the unions and their ability to tie up important public services. . . . Obviously, pressure tactics do pay off and can be expected to be used by the unions that have the necessary political strength."[9] The authors readily accept unionism in government, but their conslusions (based on field studies in nineteen communities) seriously impair the theory that the unions seek justice, equity, and fairness.

## LABOR MOBILITY

In the distant past, workers often seemed to be at the mercy of the employer. They were less mobile and less aware of better job opportunities than they are today; competition was rough at times, not only for the worker but for the investor and the enterpriser. When business fell off, or the economy went into a slump, there was a surplus of workers; they seemed to need protection. But workers, in contrast to shareholders or enterprises, were sufficiently numerous

---

8. New York, N.Y., Delacorte Press, 1968.
9. Davis T. Stanley and Carole L. Cooper. *Managing Local Government Under Union Pressure* (Washington, D.C.: © Brookings Institution, 1971).

to elicit major political sympathy, even when investors and business-men, too, underwent great stress and strain.

But things are different now. We have unemployment insurance and a nationwide employment-exchange service designed to bring job openings and job seekers together, along with a host of privately operated employment exchanges. Communications media shrink distances, enough workers are mobile and willing to respond to better employment opportunities in the next city, county, state. And the government, regardless of the party in power, is committed to the maintenance of optimum employment.

The media inform the public of economic and technical trends to guide those interested in new or different jobs and to point students, learners, and beginners in the direction that the technology and the economy are moving. Vocational counseling and education, as well as manpower-training programs, abound.

We have literally millions of employment givers. The individual may become self-employed or an employer, or he may elect to remain a job-taker. Over time, he can follow all three of these courses. He can experiment, and many, of course, do. We have no master class, no rigid or fixed upper class, no fixed middle or lower class. Upward and downward migration continues to characterize our society.[10]

Even so, most gainfully occupied persons remain job-takers throughout their lives. Yet labor-market flexibility does not require that every worker be highly mobile and flexible, always ready to shift from one occupation to another, from one place to another. The fact that some people are on the move, willing and able to experiment in new or different jobs automatically improves the position of those who are not. Marginal shifts may benefit all. The steady migration away from economic deserts and low-paying jobs improves not only the lowest and average income but also the incomes of those who make the effort to qualify for better jobs and turn out to be reliable and responsible.[11]

10. Albert Rees and G. P. Shultz in *Workers and Wages in an Urban Labor Market* conclude that the labor market is much less imperfect than commonly assumed (Chicago, Ill., University of Chicago Press, 1970).

11. For a more extended analysis of how real wages improve see *Why Wages Rise* by F.A. Harper (Irvington-on-Hudson, N.Y., Foundation for Economic Education, 1957).

# UNIONS MAY RETARD JOB-MAKING INVESTMENT

That labor unions damage the material well-being of workers is now rather widely believed. If they do slow down economic growth, they obviously hurt the working man.

Thomas Balogh, an Oxford economist, a Socialist and indeed the Chairman of the Socialist Fabian Society, turned his powerful guns on labor union officials in a tract, *Labor and Inflation.* Balogh was one of the chief authors of the Oxford Studies on which Lord Beveridge based his 1944 model for the full-employment state. He rose to high position in the Socialist Labor Party and served as economic consultant to Prime Minister Harold Wilson. Nonetheless, he ascribed the serious inflation in England to union officials, charging that they, through their unreasonable demands, have failed the workers. The twenty-five-year-record, he said, shows that un-bridled trade-union action cannot increase the workers' share of the national income. (See, *Fortune,* February 1971.) "The modern trade unionist," Balogh said, "prefers to have the cake even while preventing its baking." Strong words indeed from a Socialist!

He advised the leaders of the underdeveloped countries not to encourage the growth and power of trade unionism. In his book, *The Economics of Poverty,* he stressed the essentialness of saving and investing to improving levels of living. Trade-union officials, he noted, are generally indifferent, or even opposed, to the new capital formation that is absolutely prerequisite to rising scales of living for the workers.

All these words and ideas, coming as they do from one who is no admirer of the free-market competitive enterprise system, are in no sense antilabor, even though many union officials will cry out against them. If they came from a business executive or a business economist, some readers would be inclined to discount them; but they come from a Socialist, a Labor-Party member, a labor sympathizer.

Thus, the considerable testimony that the labor movement is counter-productive is not all partisan. Most of labor's demands are aimed at lower output, higher costs, and a shift of income to the members of the more aggressive and powerful unions. Few scholars, if any, would argue that the massive 1971 strikes in the United

States, for example, improved the equity and fairness of the wage structure throughout the economy.

In our enlightened, highly mobile age, with vigorous competition in the private sector; the *economic* usefulness of the union is minimal or even detrimental. But this does not deny that unions can perform useful noneconomic functions for their members and for society.

# THEORY X
# VERSUS
# THEORY Y

The unions' misuse of power is due, to no small extent, to an unflattering view of human nature and of man's attitude toward work. The view appears to be held by the majority of trade-union officials and by all too many business leaders. Fortunately, another view is now gaining ground in enlightened management circles and it is leading to more effective cost and quality control within the plant. Briefly, the new theory holds that most people want to work and that a major task of management is to create a work environment that will call forth the best in both employees and management.

In the terminology of Professor Douglas McGregor of MIT, the forward-looking, optimistic view is Theory Y, and the pessimistic view is Theory X.

Theory Y is the democratic, or employee-centered, approach. It assumes that employees generally do not dislike work and find the expenditure of effort to be as natural as is play or rest. Most employees will exercise some self-direction and self-control, when they are provided the opportunity, in serving the objectives they find in their job situation. Given some encouragement, employees not only accept but generally seek responsibility. The capacity to exercise imagination, ingenuity, and creativity in meeting job-situation problems, as governed by the tasks to be done, is widely, not narrowly, distributed among employees.

Employers, on an ever-widening scale, have been adopting managerial and personnel policies designed to help meet the desires, feelings, and needs of their employees, with regard not merely to

steady pay and adequate income but also to other on-the-job satisfactions—including security, ego needs, and the desire to know, to
grow, to create, and to achieve a full well-rounded experience. If
Theory Y were widely adopted, it could offset much of the damage
discussed in the foregoing chapters.

Theory X assumes that the average employee has an inherent
dislike for work and will minimize it if he can, so he must be coaxed,
controlled, directed, coerced, and threatened with punishment before he will put forth a reasonable effort. He prefers to be directed,
wishes to avoid responsibility, has little ambition, and, above all,
wants security. The employers and union officials who accept
Theory X have a low opinion of the worker. The union leaders, in
particular, view work as inherently unpleasant, something to be
performed grudgingly.

Professors Arthur A. Thompson and Irwin Weinstock examined
the literature on labor in this context and published a report,
"Facing the Crisis in Collective Bargaining."[1] They prepared the
accompanying chart (Chart 8) to provide a quick overview of the
striking contrast between Theory X and Theory Y. It merits careful
study, particularly by business executives and managers of enterprises, whether large or small.

Douglas McGregor is particularly critical of business executives
who blame their employees and their business associates for low
productivity, low morale, etc. He concludes that the businessman
who plays by ear and relies on his own long experience (however
successful) often has a false theory of human nature, one that will
get him into trouble.[2] Every managerial act, he insists, rests on
assumptions, generalizations, and hypotheses—that is to say, on
theory, and theory and practice are inseparable. To believe otherwise
is fatal. McGregor develops evidence to support his conception of the
multisided dimensions of human nature and to show how it is
possible to combine the worker's self-interest with the needs of the
employing establishment and its organization to the benefit of all. He

---

1. *Michigan State University Business Topics*, East Lansing, Mich., Summer
1968.

2. Douglas McGregor. *The Human Side of Enterprise* (New York. N.Y.:
McGraw-Hill, 1960).

provides numerous striking illustrations of both right and wrong theory-practice. Once management at all levels fully grasps the notion of the effective integration of the interests of employees, management, and shareholders, the way is paved for improved performance, including effective cost control.

Unfortunately, McGregor does not deal adequately with the complications created by the pressures, strategy, and tactics of union officials, whose primary concern appears to be the maintenance of their own prestige and emoluments of office. They assume the adversary stance as a survival tactic, and tend to view the employer-employee relationship as ipso facto antagonistic. McGregor shows how to help offset this "unnatural" tendency.

The Theory Y manager, believing that the employee's job can be intrinsically rewarding and attractive, will attempt to provide him with opportunities to satisfy his multiple needs on the job. In contrast, the union official will strive for a contract package providing economic satisfactions that materialize *away from* the job, stressing higher pay, more fringes, shorter hours, longer vacations, and sabbatical leaves, as well as various forms of job security. In a single sentence, the AFL-CIO leadership shows its aversion to work: "We shall seek reduced schedules of working hours, additional paid holidays, longer vacations, sabbatical leaves, early retirement and similar provisions. . . ." (*Policy Resolutions,* 1969.) Union officials frequently oppose voluntary efforts of Theory Y managers to provide broader job satisfactions, lest they weaken the loyalty of the workers to the union.[3]

Economic benefits wrested from employers by violence and strikes provide the thoughtful worker with little genuine satisfaction, and often with some feeling of guilt and wrongdoing. This explains, in part, the surly attitude of some unionized employees and their rude treatment of the public. Yet it would be a mistake to conclude that a union can serve no useful purpose. It can, and frequently does, meet a genuine human need, that of protecting the individual worker from

---

3. Lemuel R. Boulware, in *The Truth About Baulwarism* (Washington, D.C.: Bureau of National Affairs, 1969), is replete with references to the "material and nonmaterial" values of the job. C.J. Dover in *Management Communications on Controversial Issues* (same publisher, 1965) stresses similar themes.

## CHART 8

### EXAMPLES OF THE LOGIC AND STRATEGIES OF THEORY X-ORIENTED UNIONS AND THEORY Y-ORIENTED MANAGEMENTS*

| Union Strategy (Theory X) | Union Logic (Theory X) | ← Topic → | Management Logic (Theory Y) | Management Strategy (Theory Y) |
|---|---|---|---|---|
| Seek shorter workweek, longer vacations. Base pay upon hours, not production. Fight "speed-ups." | Inherently unpleasant, avoid where possible. | The worker's job. | Can be intrinsically attractive and rewarding. People seek intellectual and physical expression. | Provide attainable satisfactions of multiple needs through work. Integrate the goals of the organization with those of workers. |
| Seek higher wages, more fringes, tenure rights, job and earnings guarantees, job training, utilize grievance procedure to ensure fair treatment. | The prime current motivator, the highest level human need of direct concern to unions. To be satisfied even at the cost of ego and development satisfactions. | The worker's economic security. | A fundamental need, often substantially satisfied in our affluent economy, at which point higher level needs are strongly activated. | Provide normal fringes. Stress development of personal skills and productivity as the best form of economic security. As workers achieve a sense of economic security, then seek to provide opportunities for satisfying ego and personal development needs. |

| | | | | |
|---|---|---|---|---|
| Stress fair and equal treatment, except for seniority privileges. Minimize management power to treat workers as individuals. | Of small concern. Best satisfied off the job. Efforts to differentiate among workers may jeopardize their economic security as well as unity within the bargaining unit. | Ego needs. (Desire for self-confidence, self-esteem, integrity, independence, etc.) Development needs. | Self-esteem and respect of others are powerful, insatiable needs. Intelligent management can integrate ego satisfactions with high productivity. | Upgrade skills, enlarge jobs, use general supervision, encourage individual responsibility, recognition, and participation of workers in managerial decisions. |
| Nonexistent. | Generally unrecognized. | (Desire to grow, to create, to achieve full inherent potential.) | Desire for personal development evolves spontaneously as basic needs are satisfied. Job performance and personal growth can be quite compatible. | Same as above |

*Arthur A. Thompson and Irwin Weinstock, "Facing the Crisis in Collective Bargaining," *MSU Business Topics*, Summer 1968. Reprinted with permission of the publisher, Division of Research, Graduate School of Business Administration, Michigan State University.

arbitrary and capricious authority, particularly from the foremen. Professor Lloyd G. Reynolds of Yale, one of the nation's leading labor economists, recently observed that the most important function of unionism is the defense of the individual worker against arbitrary treatment by supervisory officials.[4] The books by Boulware, Dover, and McGregor merit wide study at all management levels.[5]

## REDUCING OUTPUT AND RAISING COSTS

Nearly everyone and every family want more income. Yet union officials favor restraints on the production needed to create this "more." Why this contradiction? And not only union officials. The government itself—despite its commitment in the Employment Act of 1946 to maximize employment, production, and purchasing power under free enterprise—carries on many anti-output programs and policies in agriculture, in foreign trade, in use of resources, in labor legislation, in strike control, and in a host of other areas. At ceremonies marking the opening of a new passenger-ship terminal in New York in 1971, Helen D. Bentley, chairman of the Federal Maritime Commission, critically analyzed what had gone wrong on the ship docks:

> Even though we all intensely dislike discussing unpleasantries on special occasions such as this, I feel that I must point out that a principal reason for the ultimate demise of the American-flag passenger ships was the labor problem— literally overstaffing and the refusal of well-paid crew members to turn to when needed, and insistence on overtime payments for performing just ordinary tasks during their regular shifts. The costs became phenomenal. . . .
> If the baggage handlers, storers of the foodstuffs on board the cruise ships, and other dockworkers turn to and

---

4. See his *The Three Worlds of Economics* (New Haven, Conn.: Yale University Press, 1971, p. 45).

5. The remainder of this chapter is based, in part, on an article by the author appearing in *Missouri Business,* Jefferson City, Mo., February 1967.

perform in stellar fashion whenever they are called upon to work, this terminal cannot help but be a success. The shipowners will want to continue returning here to pick up cruise passengers. But if the costs are run up ridiculously high because of deliberate stalling, burdensome work rules, and determination by the men *not* to put their shoulders to the wheel, then even the new $37 million facility will be forced to fail.

As the commissioner pointed out, the United States cannot possibly remain the leading industrial nation of the world if the dock policies are allowed to extend to all industries:

Nobody ever thought the American-flag passenger ship would become a thing of the past, but it has on the East Coast and soon will be on the West Coast. Just as that happened so could this new passenger terminal fail if the dockers fail to restore pride in their work and become fully productive citizens. Pride and productivity not only helped make the port of New York the world's leading port for years, but those two factors also helped make the United States the greatest industrial nation in the world.

If a nation's leaders are incapable of learning the hard lessons of such facts as these, perhaps that nation deserves to go into eclipse.

But again we must not exaggerate. Reducing the workweek is not necessarily bad, and the reduction might be a matter of degree. For example, our forebears worked from sunrise to sunset, six or seven days a week. Gradually, beginning about 130 years ago, the workweek was shortened. The twelve- and the ten-hour day are things of the past, but no legislation, or unions, were responsible for the contraction. Perhaps the owners and supervisors disliked having their own noses to the grindstone so long at a time. The eight-hour day was adopted in the last quarter of the nineteenth century in a few occupations, largely without legislation or widespread unionism. Rising productivity has increased the relative value of leisure, besides making more of it possible.

Restrictions on output, particularly since 1930, often in the name of fringe benefits or "social gains," have been less spontaneous. They appear to be due to an assortment of forces: man's alleged allergy to work, contagious spread of counterproduction ideas, laws and union practices designed to spread the work (camouflaging unemployment), well-meaning but often ill-advised government schemes to help the weak, the poor, and often the not-so-poor, and finally the politician's and union official's need to come up with some new salable restrictions. All these have played a role in raising costs and lowering output, providing more time off than the majority of workers may really want.

Consider the likely impact of the following typical union demands:

| UNION DEMANDS | LIKELY IMPACT | |
| --- | --- | --- |
| | *Higher Costs* | *Reduced Output & Higher Costs* |
| 1. Shorter workweek | | X |
| 2. More paid holidays | | X |
| 3. Longer paid vacations | | X |
| 4. Periodic 3-month leaves | | X |
| 5. Day off before or after paid holiday | | X |
| 6. Full pay for birthday anniversary | | X |
| 7. Restrictions on output | | X |
| 8. Opposition to labor-saving machinery | | X |
| 9. Decelerated installation of labor-saving machinery | | X |
| 10. Opposition to new and better materials or processes | | X |
| 11. Opposition to relocating production to more efficient places and plants | | X |
| 12. Opposition to contracting-out maintenance and other work | | X |
| 13. Coffee breaks | X | X(?) |
| 14. Portal to portal pay | X | |

| UNION DEMANDS | LIKELY IMPACT | |
| --- | --- | --- |
| | *Higher Costs* | *Reduced Output & Higher Costs* |
| 15. Paid wash-up and clean-up time | X | |
| 16. Supplementary unemployment pay | X | |
| 17. Severance pay | X | |
| 18. Compulsory hiring of unneeded workers | | X |
| 19. Life and health insurance | X | |
| 20. Pensions | X | |
| 21. Higher pay for same output | X | |
| 22. Cost-of-living escalators | X | |
| 23. Free or subsidized lunches and similar items | X | |
| 24. Guaranteed annual wages | X | |
| 25. Penalties on overtime | | X |
| 26. Premiums on early retirement | | X |
| 27. Compulsory minimum wage rates | | X |

This list is not exhaustive. Is it not remarkable that every one of these demands should either reduce output, or raise costs, or both?

The union official (and his political ally) is typically indifferent to rising costs and lowered output. His myopic view of the good life is to do less and collect more for the less. The more the union official achieves toward these two goals, the "better" he views his own performance.

Not all of these demands are necessarily bad. Why, for example, should a man now be on the job sixty, seventy or seventy-five hours a week? All work and no play is a dull routine. Why, if workingmen generally prefer more leisure, and also steady, uniform, weekly pay envelopes, shouldn't they be paid for vacations or holidays? If workingmen can't, or don't muster the self-discipline to save for a rainy day, should not voluntary arrangements be made to withhold, in effect, part of their pay to set up pension and life- and health-insurance schemes? Coffee breaks may be a way to enhance efficiency, not just a habit that is often abused. It's a matter of degree.

Union officials constantly lament their inferior public image.[6] But if they want to improve it, the prescription is simple: reverse the slogan once in a while—stop demanding more money for less output and more pay for fewer hours; oppose strikes and threats of violence and run union affairs as democratically and openly as is possible. No high-level IQ or training is needed to perceive that we can consume only that which we first produce. Few working men or their families have as much as they would like to consume; human wants are endless.

Once the basic needs for food, apparel, and shelter are met, the need for better and more varied food rapidly emerges; the same is true of apparel and shelter. Our existing wants for recreation, entertainment, sports, dental and health care, trips at home or abroad, summer retreats, cultural and educational advantages vastly exceed our present productive capacities. It is simply not true that there is only a fixed amount of work to be done.

Every reduction of output or cost-raising step "gained" by one union tends to place a burden on all other workers. Workers, in our exchange economy, work primarily one for another, not for the employer.

## PRODUCTIVITY AND THEORY Y

Rising costs are reflected in prices. Considering the long list of output-reduction practices engaged in by unions, with government sanction, it is surprising that we have attained as much general affluence as we have. How come? In a few words: competition and the rewards for the new and the better. We owe our rising per capita output primarily to better education, to science, invention, research, new technology, new processes, improved machinery, saving, high-grade innovative entrepreneurship, and risk-taking—all these have

---

6. Disbelief in U. S. institutions has grown, with organized labor near the bottom of the list. *Business Week*, June 17, 1972, p. 100.

combined to minimize costs, to provide better values, and to pass the fruits on to the consumer.

Production and innovative incentives and competition don't sound exceptionally glamorous. They make little fuss or public noise. Yet on tens of thousands of fronts hidden from public view, they increase the production yield per hour, and the bulk of the gains are translated by competition in the market, step by step, into better consumer values, even though the process is obscured by the government's pro-inflation policies.

The artificial hurdles and barriers to more output per hour are immense and are raised from year to year; yet creative effort is not a relic of the past. Incentives to excel are alive and lively. Competition passes on more benefits to the common man than to the uncommon man whose saving and investing bring about most of the rise in productivity.[7]

Dr. John W. Kendrick, a leading student of productivity, tells us that since 1966 there has been a pronounced slowdown in the rate of productivity growth. Yet he is convinced that "the vast majority of Americans desire rising real incomes—judging from union demands and the search by individuals for better pay, the savings habits of individuals who seek to increase their property incomes, and the continued pressures on governments at all levels to provide more and better services."[8]

Productivity can be expressed as a ratio, the relation of (1) *inputs*, such as labor, management, capital, energy, improvement in method, process, and raw material, etc., and (2) the *output*. Changes in productivity reflect the changes in this ratio over a period of time. We are getting more for our inputs, according to Dr. Kendrick, but the rate of improvement is slipping, due primarily to reduced rates of spending on research and development, disturbances to productivity

---

7. In a Congressional Hearing, Senator J. K. Javits asked George Meany for specific proposals on productivity improvements, but Meany refused to answer. See *Congressional Record,* April 25, 1972, p. S 6644.

8. See "The Productivity Slowdown," *Business Economics,* September 1971, Washington, D.C. *Business Week,* September 9, 1972 devotes pp. 79-150 to our productivity lag and makes many constructive suggestions. (Reprints are available for $1 each, 1221 Avenue of the Americas, New York, N.Y. 10020.

from inflation, an enormous increase in government regulatory interventions, increased expenditures for environmental and ecological purposes, and the recent emergence of the hippie and similar subcultures. He is obviously doubtful of our return to the former annual average rate of productivity improvement so long as Theory X continues to dominate the thinking of union leaders. Actually, there is a negative correlation between the degree of unionization of industries and the rates of productivity improvement. In trying to achieve the goal of all members getting more, the labor union has, on net balance, been counterproductive.

The alacrity with which the four-day, forty-hour workweek is being embraced is disturbing in this context. Psychologists and others "proved" in days of yore that the eight-hour workday is better than a ten-hour workday. Does it follow that a four-day, thirty-hour workweek would be still better, or that it would gratify the workers themselves? (Or their wives?) The prevalence of moonlighting indicates that many workers prefer more work and income to more leisure. And output would almost certainly decline due to gross underutilization of land and other natural resources; of factory and other space; and of costly, potentially productive equipment. A thirty-hour week of utilization may result in more than 82 percent idle time.

Even under the standard forty-hour, five-day workweek, the average actual workweek (hours on the job) is already under thirty-five hours. This is due to paid holidays, paid vacations, paid sick leave, paid personal-birthday time off, paid time for jury duty, for funerals, for the day before or after a holiday, and for a host of other no-work periods dreamed up by the exponents of Theory X.

Antisocial reductions of output, and the practices of governments and unions that favor restrictions and raise costs, damage all of us as workers and consumers. The need is not so much for harder work, as for more productive teamwork, more "total-factor productivity," as Kendrick puts it, and more careful control of our cost increases, for the benefit of all users and consumers, here and abroad.

A single issue of *Memo from Cope* (February 14, 1972) of the AFL-CIO carried these four scary headlines:

182

The Vicious Vise on Workers—exported Jobs, Imported Goods.

Made in America? . . . Not Very Likely.

American Industrial Power in Ohio? Pa.? Ill.? Calif.? Look Again . . .

It's France. (Map of France showing USA plant installations.) "Made in America" . . . It's a vanishing slogan.

Then followed a heated plea for restraining our foreign investments, punishing earnings abroad, reducing imports. This is a fairly recent stance for this labor federation but one that many of its constituent unions now endorse and urge.

The massive pressures for higher import duties, for import quotas and for temporary surcharge taxes on imports (adopted in 1971), and the opposition to our multinational companies—all these result in great part from costs and prices that are out of line with those abroad and from the popular belief that employment opportunities are limited. Some politicians and some business executives, as well as most union officials, cry for protection. But this is a game foreign nations can play with equal or even greater skill!

The realignment of our currency with foreign currencies beginning in mid-August 1971 was forced upon us primarily by the egregious mistakes of our government, and the power of the unions.[9] Unless we curb that power, currency realignment will be only a temporary palliative. This is a point that is far more important than these few words imply.

We do face a crisis in collective bargaining. If it is to be allayed, business executives must energetically pursue Theory Y policies and practices; unions must be shorn of the powers that now make it so difficult to wean them away from their attachment to Theory X.

---

9. Obviously a number of things, besides government policies in regard to labor unions and collective bargaining, have gone wrong; but this study is concerned primarily with improved labor and personnel policies, in which much un-doing by government is required.

# TOWARD A
# NEW POLICY
# ON UNION MONOPOLY
# AND WAGE
# SETTLEMENTS

Throughout this book many suggestions for dealing with the undue market power of the labor union have been made. It is neither necessary nor possible to repeat and fully justify here again all the proposals or obvious corrective steps.

Those who are dedicated to human freedom and liberty, and to the philosophy of limited government will not carelessly recommend more government, or more controls over human action and freedom. Yet obviously some things have gone badly wrong in our society. Government has built up labor-union power to the point where government itself simply does not know how to restrain it. This is true in Western countries generally.

More and more objective observers—some of them Socialists—concur on the dire need to disperse the power of the union official and the labor union, if collective bargaining is to be really free.

The labor market has been discussed only in broad, general terms. Actually, in every state and in every city, we have a series of different or noncompeting labor markets. For example, the labor markets in the printing trades and the news media vary enormously among themselves, and from the labor markets in the local construction industry. All of those differ widely from those in the steel industry, or in the automobile-manufacturing industry, or in transportation.

## DISPERSING UNDUE POWER

The basic goal of reform in all labor markets is the same—dispersing undue union power. The specific remedies suitable for the highly variegated markets will, however, vary. How deal with the strike of fifteen garage mechanics who closed down a major newspaper, *The Evening Star* (Washington, D.C.), in contrast to a tugboat strike in a harbor, an East Coast dockworkers strike, or a nationwide railroad strike? Employers, who must deal with the union officials, do not agree as to methods. They and their industry associations should give more study to the matter.

What legal limits should be placed on union demands? Union officials virtually always insist on complete freedom—no limits. Thus, James R. Hoffa, former president of the Teamsters Union said, upon his release from a penitentiary in December 1971, "I feel that any restriction on labor activities, other than in time of war, are not in the interest of working men and women."[1]

Government has literally lost its sovereign power in regard to this matter. George Meany bluntly defied the idea of any government control over illegal strikes in an extended interview in 1972. Here is how it went:

Q. Will something have to be done about the question of strikes among public employees? Do you feel that that is an area where the right to strike needs to be preserved?

A. Well, they don't have the right to strike, by law.

Q. But they do strike—

A. They do strike. That's my answer.
   The union leaders keep coming to me and say, "We ought to have someone put a bill in to give us the right to strike." And I say, "What for? You strike when you feel you have to strike."
   Even the postal people—what happens when they strike? If the strike is effective, public officials negotiate a settlement—that's what happens.

---

1. *Washington Post,* Washington, D.C., January 3, 1972.

Q. Do you think there ought to be compulsory arbitration in that field, as an alternative to just saying "no strikes?"

A. No.[2]

And, proud as Meany was of the defiance of the postal workers, this was his answer to the more timid union officials who wanted a law passed to make sure that government workers have the "right" to strike. He was not in the least concerned for the welfare of those who depend on the prompt, daily delivery of the mail. Have these people equal rights for continuity of mail delivery? The record of such defiance is extensive. The case for the dispersal of monopoly power—literally, a form of dictatorial power—strengthens with each passing month.

Peter Wiles struggled valiantly, though somewhat indecisively, with the issue. Considering all the relevant evidence, as he saw it, he concluded that trade unions should be abolished, even as he asked himself about the wisdom of recommending the politically improbable. His answer was interesting:

> Quite the contrary. The unions must be shocked out of their easy consciences. They must see that, at present, their sole justification is social inertia. It is only their prior *être* that is their *raison d'être,* and all the high-flown arguments they use are false. They have no moral *locus standi,* and are but a necessary evil. Give them a bad conceit of themselves, and then they will be more inclined to do their plain duty.

A careful reading of his article (*Encounter,* September 1956) is strongly urged. Anyone who studies this meticulous, sympathetic analysis may never again be quite the same person.

Employees, just like Rotarians, Jaycees, business executives, and professional people, should surely be allowed to assemble and associate freely in organizations of their own choosing—provided, of course, that their aims, purposes and methods are within the law. Such voluntary associations provide a sense of community.

---

2. Copyrighted interview in *U. S. News and World Report,* February 21, 1972.

Government interferes massively in the affairs and conduct of business, and rarely does anyone regard this invasion of business decision-making as unconstitutional—although much of it is foolish, childish, and counterproductive.[3] This invasion is *people control,* and to disperse union power also will be *people control.* Both types of controls are justifiable on both philosophic and economic grounds. Wisely conceived, they can make the free competitive market work more effectively to the benefit of the consumer.

## ABOLISHING STRIKES

Government activities and enterprises generally continue operations without interruption, unless the employees stop them. Public utilities and enterprises "effected with a public interest" may not turn down customers, discontinue any phase of their activities, or close down their enterprises without authorization from a public-

---

3. A book such as that by Donald S. Watson, *Economic Policy: Business and Government* (op. cit.) provides countless instances of government interferences with business, based on common law, statutory law, court decisions, and above all a host of administrative rules and regulations by commissions, bureaus, authorities, divisions, agencies, etc., at the national, state, and local levels. Many of these apply to all business generally (where relevant), such as antitrust, including mergers, acquisitions, divestitures, interlocking directorships, dealership relations, franchising, promotion, advertising, quantity discounts and other pricing policies; minimum and prevailing wages; compulsory union recognition and bargaining; railways financing strikes against themselves; flotation of securities, securities exchanges, and buying and selling securities by company officers; packaging, labeling, and spelling out endless specifications of soaps, detergents, cosmetics, and almost everything else (a court order·prevented the use of the Esso gasoline label in twenty states); hiring policies as to race, ethnic group, sex, age; so-called unfair methods of competition designed to succor weaklings; price policies, promotion, loss leaders, etc.; zoning laws—the list is endless.

In addition, many lines of business are singled out by separate laws for additional special treatment and attention: pharmaceutical manufacture and distribution; radio and television; public utilities, whose rates of return are government-dictated as are their pricing structures; certificates of convenience and necessity required at times of utilities, compulsory service of utilities, including railways and pipelines; building controls, including codes—often conflicting local, state, and national (FHA, VA, HUD in general); insurance; finan-

188

service commission. (*Munn vs. Ill.,* 94 U.S. 111, 1876.) This principle has held for several hundred years.[4]

Yet strikes against public utilities, which themselves must continue to operate, are usually quite legal. The employer must do the operating; the employees need not. What a travesty of justice, equity, and equal treatment by the law! A public indifferent to this travesty gets what it deserves; if the resulting disorder and inconvenience finally leads to dictatorship, the people will have only themselves to blame.

What of newspaper strikes? The Pittsburgh papers were struck in late 1970 and early 1971, and again on May 14, 1971. They were closed down—this time for more than 125 days. The damage, harm, and inconvenience to tens of thousands of people were enormous. James J. Kilpatrick, in a column entitled "What Kind of Newsman Shuts Down His Paper?" wondered at the servility of his fellow craftsmen in the newspaper trade. "What has become of pride, duty, devotion?" Once these words held deep meaning. But in the *Evening Star* strike, the reporters, writers and subeditors surrendered like sheep to a handful of auto mechanics. A strike, said Kilpatrick, should arise only from terrible provocations, out of serious exploita-

---

cial institutions including building and loan associations, banks, mortgage companies, mutual funds, etc.; packers and stockyards; other food processors; burial and cremation; trade associations; cigarette advertising (in spite of the First Amendment); automotive design and specifications; a vast product safety panoply; import quotas and export licenses; international capital movements and repatriation of earnings; transportation; real estate; petroleum mining, refining, and distribution; other mining; lumbering; barbering; brewing; distilling; hospital construction and operation.

Again, the list is endless; some of the interventions may well be justified, for example, the interventions in business for environmental, ecological, and similar reasons. The point of this digression is to show plenty of precedents, if government should desire to eliminate the monopoly power of the labor union.

The low opinion of the consumer held by the legislator is shown by Dr. G. J. Stigler, "The Economic Role of the State," in *The New Argument in Economics,* eds. Helmut Schoeck and J. W. Wiggins (New York, N.Y.: D. Van Nostrand, 1963). See also the book by Mary B. Peterson in this Series, *The Regulated Consumer,* 1972.

4. Roscoe Pound, *Labor Unions and the Concept of Public Service* (Washington, D.C.: American Enterprise Institute, 1959).

tion, real injustice, wretched and dangerous conditions of work, a palpable and deliberate effort by management to destroy a union.[5]

Whether Mr. Kilpatrick intended to extend this limitation on striking to all types of enterprises, he did not say. But morality and ethics are not matters of numbers; who, for example, is the least moral—the man who murders one person or the man who murders two, or twenty-two?

A strike against a filling station, a retailer, a book publisher, or a candlestick-maker damages people: owners, those who want to work, consumers. A strike against a toy maker, in late summer or early fall of the year, or against the builders of an office building scheduled for opening at a specific date[6], hurts many innocent people. It impairs *their* freedom, *their* dignity, *their* commitments to others. It may destroy the economic value of their services and their assets. They too have feelings and sensitivity. Do they have a right *not* to be struck against? Surely the equal protection of the law does not stop with public utilities and government activities. If the so-called right to strike were eliminated, the right for an individual to quit would remain unimpaired, except as contracts for the performance of services require a continuation of employment relations.

Regarding the stress and discomfort caused by strikes *to employees themselves,* George Meany said, "More and more people in the trade-union movement . . . are thinking of other ways to advance without the use of the strike method." O. G. Stahl, long-time director of the Civil Service Commission's Bureau of Policies and Standards, published an article "The Case Against Strikes" in *Good Government* (Winter 1970 and condensed in *Reader's Digest,* October 1971). He urged arbitration and other substitutes for the strike and quoted I. W. Abel of the Steelworkers Union as saying, "The strike is obsolete." He also urged that employers make an effort to keep wages and salaries in line with the open market, a point developed later.

---

5. *Evening Star,* Washington, D.C., January 12, 1971.

6. For an account of a horrible miscarriage of justice in the erection of a United States office building in Buffalo, N.Y., see *Time,* August 30, 1971, p. 21. For a strong case against the "right to strike" see, Leonard E. Read, *The Coming Aristocracy* (Irvington-on-Hudson, N.Y. : Foundation for Economic Education, 1969). A part of this is reproduced in the Appendix to this chapter.

Labor unions are not exclusively economic warriors with the sole function of wresting greater sums from employers (consumers). Wherever people play, consort, or work together there will be *people* problems. Youngsters playing baseball in a vacant lot must have rules of the game, and they must have umpires or rulers. Acceptance of rules is necessary. Differences among people in the same game, or working under the same roof, require continuous accommodation to agreed-upon and evolving rules. An association among employees to develop acceptable customs, practices, and standards is desirable and probably inevitable. Disputes among employees are numerous, but many can best be resolved by the accepted policies of their own association. Disputes with the supervisors and employers are likewise inevitable; machinery is needed to resolve them as well. All this is obvious, and requires no further elaboration.

The damage done by unionism in action derives primarily from three sources: (1) excessive union preoccupation with Theory X, as noted in Chapter XIII (2) the legal immunities, the special privileges of unions, and the massive economic power of unions in collective bargaining, and (3) the failure of employers to resolutely carry out the policies associated with Theory Y.[7]

Employers have been highly remiss in this last aspect, and many seem to deserve what they get from the unions—but the consumer, who is the ultimate victim of Theory X error, suffers most from the neglect and recalcitrance of the employers.


## LEGAL IMMUNITIES OF LABOR UNIONS

The special immunities and privileges extended to unions and their officials (as described in detail by Dean Roscoe Pound) need to be withdrawn or corrected. Labor unions should be required to incorporate and to take full responsibility for contract compliance and for damage done by their leaders, their hired agents, *and* their members. They should be placed in a position no worse, and no better, than

---

7. For related literature see numerous sources cited in "Whither Human Resource Management in the Seventies?" by F. G. Lippert in *Michigan Business Review,* March 1972, Ann Arbor, Mich.

management people are placed in. Injunctive relief should be restored by repeal of the Norris-LaGuardia Act of 1932; the same is true of similar state laws, local ordinances, and practices that have grown up since the 1930s.

Dr. Edward H. Chamberlin maintained that if the public is to be protected from irresponsible monopoly union power, a body of antitrust law appropriate to the labor markets has an importance at least equal to that taken for granted in the product market, even though the existing antitrust law cannot be made fully applicable to labor markets. The fact that labor costs account for about 75 percent of all costs speaks volumes about the importance of competition in the labor market, interstate and intrastate.

Output restriction by a union generally escapes legal penalties. Featherbedding and massively uneconomic work practices are found in construction, printing, transportation, and a host of other trades. Apart from matters of health and safety, all such restrictiveness should be outlawed, and firmly enforced.

The scope of control by most unions should be greatly reduced, but even here employers themselves may figure that if their competitors are hit by the same union demands, they will all be in the same boat—none suffers comparatively or overwhelmingly. But this is not true if, in collusion, management and labor get an industry's costs so high that jobs are artificially exported abroad, or the consumer turns to substitutes, or our international payments become so out of balance that our currency becomes unacceptable abroad, as it did in the summer of 1971, and we are forced into a serious retreat from freer international trade—as we have been.

Downward valuation of the dollar (relative to the currency of other countries) will be helpful only temporarily if we allow unrestricted wage increases and uneconomic work practices to continue in both exporting and nonexporting industries. Export markets may be lost; *and* we, in turn, may buy more abroad because of relatively better import values. So employers in a broad range of industries, their employees, and their families have a strong personal, individual interest in reducing uneconomic work practices and avoiding monopoly wage settlements. Improving the competitive standing of our industries is in the interest of nearly all workers and consumers.

Employers should develop alternative sources of supply, where

192

feasible, to enlarge the range of their choices. The National Labor Relations Act should be repealed, since it was founded on a major mis-diagnosis of the nature of our depression problems in the 1930s. Short of outright repeal, the NLRB should be restricted to conducting so-called collective bargaining elections to determine the appropriate bargaining unit.[8]

But here too a further major correction is now urgent. The law requires that "Employees shall have the right to organize and bargain collectively through representatives of their own choosing. . . ." If any such language is retained at all, it should be changed to read ". . . representatives of their own choosing, selected *from among the employees of their own employer*. . . ." The individual employer would no longer have to deal with strangers whom he never hired, doesn't know and doesn't want to know. Employers accustomed to the present system could still bargain with these strangers, but the law would not and should not require them to do so.

The goal should be *local* wage settlements, avoiding company-wide settlements in multiplant enterprises.

That 51 percent of the voting employees select a given union as their bargaining agent should not prevent the other 49 percent from bargaining individually, or from selecting another union. Compulsory union membership should be outlawed. Always, the goal should be to disperse monopoly power, and thereby eradicate coercion.

The ultimate coercive weapon of the union is not the strike, but violence, actual or potential. With the national government invading the field of industrial relations through the National Labor Relations Act and many other laws, we encounter a major anachronism. The central government dictates the rules of collective bargaining, but state and local governments are primarily responsible for the protection of life and property. Thus violence, coercion, arson, threats to life, limb, and property may be widely used whenever a struck employer tries to operate.[9] To humanize industrial relations, every

---

8. The NLRB has approved "authorization cards" as evidence of union sentiment. For exposure of this "Buttonhole Ballot" see *Wall Street Journal* editorial, October 6, 1971.

9. Judge Gerard D. Reilly, former member of NLRB, has written an excellent piece on "States Rights and the Law of Labor Relations," in *Labor Unions and Public Policy* (Washington, D.C., American Enterprise Institute, 1958).

layer of government—national, state, and local—must steel itself in a maximum effort and determination to stamp out all private use of force and violence. Under these circumstances collective bargaining could serve a useful purpose.[10]

If government will not enforce the law against violence and coercion, or trespass and creating a nuisance, obstructing traffic, etc., injured individuals can bring appropriate legal action against local and state officials. In addition, they could bring private actions against union officials as well as against the union members who do the damage through illegal acts to persons and property. The law of torts could be brought into use.

A powerful aggressive union can retaliate against the government, or one law, or one lawsuit, and inflict more damage than it receives. But striking against a hundred different plaintiffs exercising their legal rights under different laws concerning illegal trade-union activity might give pause even to a tough union official. Michael G. Bell made this point in connection with the coal miners' strike in the United Kingdom in 1972. He suggested that if a small fraction of the people who were intimidated, were forcibly prevented from doing their jobs, using their own property, or fulfilling their contracts had identified the offenders and had at once taken legal action against them, the situation might have been altered markedly for the better. Companies under contract to make deliveries at the power stations could also have taken effective legal action.[11]

"Collective clobbering," to use the phrase of *The Economist,* must go. Then the number of uneconomic wage settlements will decrease, our international balance-of-payments problems would be mitigated, and inflation would be less of a problem—although, as noted elsewhere, the prime and fundamental cause of inflation is excessive government spending and irresponsible fiscal and monetary policy.

10. There would remain much hassle and counterproductive activity in many cases. During the General Motors-UAW negotiations in the fall of 1970 some 39,000 grievances were advanced by the union, mostly local issues. So unrewarding were these negotiations that the last plant did not go back to work until January 23, 1971, although the national agreement was signed on November 11, 1970, after a long and costly strike. See *Nation's Business,* October 1971, interview with James M. Roche, chairman of GM.

11. *The Economist,* London, March 4, 1972, p. 4.

Inflation is a major inducement to more militant collective bargaining.

## RISING? STABLE? OR FALLING AVERAGE PRICES?

The idea that average prices should remain level, but wages and salaries should forever march upward is almost universally held. Does this make it right? Or economically correct?

Does anyone know by how much employee remuneration should rise next year? Can government pronounce annually in advance what the average rise should be? Actually, this was done in the 1960s with very dubious results.[12] The Pay Board in 1971 set a target of 5.5 percent increases per year, but settlements in coal, railways, aerospace, dockwork, and others, massively pierced the ceiling.

As early as January 1960, *The Economic Report of the President* seemed to endorse the idea of a target wage settlement:

> ... settlements should not be such as to cause the national average of wage-rate increases to exceed sustainable rates of improvement in national productivity. A national wage pattern that fails to meet this criterion would put an upward pressure on the price level. Hourly rates of pay and related labor benefits can, of course, be increased without jeopardizing price stability. Indeed, such increases are the major means in our free economy by which labor shares in the fruits of industrial progress.

As a general statement, this is sound enough (although the last sentence is historically inaccurate). And surely we need to understand better the relations between productivity and wage settlements, and average prices. Nor should we be indifferent to the inequities created by secularly rising average money wages. But to an employer, or a union official, how meaningful is the above advice, or the following as a guide in a specific case?

---

12. For perhaps the best short analysis of the failures see *Essays on Inflation* by George Terborgh, particularly the first essay (Washington, D.C.: Machinery and Allied Products Institute, 1971).

But improvements in compensation rates must, on the average, remain within the limits of general productivity gains if reasonable stability of prices is to be achieved and maintained. Furthermore, price reductions warranted by especially rapid productivity gains must be a normal and frequent feature of our economy. Without such reductions we shall not be able to keep the price level *as a whole* from advancing.

Similar ideas have been advanced in other countries by governments, as well as by private spokesmen. Yet, after more careful exploration numerous doubts have arisen. For example, in its first report published in 1958, the Council on Prices, Productivity, and Incomes (appointed by the Government of the United Kingdom in August 1957) pointed to the dangers of an advance announcement for an annual money wage increase as standard practice, and came to some constructive conclusions on wage settlements:

> We must revert at this point to the suggestion that from time to time a percentage figure should be announced by which average money wages could increase during the year without damage to the national interest. We are conscious of the attractiveness of this proposal, offering as it does the hope of establishing a link between the rate of wage increases and the growth in over-all productivity. There are, however, serious practical objections to it. There would always be industries in which there were good reasons for the advance in wages to exceed the average; others in which much less good reasons for it to do so could be thought up; very few in which the case for lagging behind the average would be readily conceded.

Then, applying these findings, the Council stated:

> There would thus be a real danger that the prescribed average would always become a minimum, and the process of wage inflation therefore built into the system. This is apart from the point . . . that such a procedure seems to involve too definite an endorsement of the doctrine that in a progressive community the *general* level of prices should never be permitted or encouraged to fall as an alternative to a rise in money income.[13]

---

13. *First Report,* London, Her Majesty's Stationery Office, 1958.

Although these words of warning were issued in the late 1950s, our Council of Economic Advisers completely ignored them, apparently assuming that union officials would not employ their energy, power, and drive to wrest the maximum feasible amounts from the employers (consumers).

Many scholars in the United States had previously issued appropriate warnings. Professor Walter A. Morton of the University of Wisconsin expressed strong doubts about the usefulness of exploratory annual conferences early in the year, as proposed by Professor John T. Dunlop of Harvard; these were supported by President Dwight Eisenhower and the AFL-CIO officials. Morton said:

> . . . in a free society standards of reasonable wages, prices and profits cannot be determined independently of the processes of competition and bargaining. I submit that even a job-conscious theory of the labor movement, fully implemented by pure theory, statistics and econometrics, cannot tell us what particular wages and prices ought to be. This is because in a free society price is a consequence of competition and bargaining, not a guide to what such competition and bargaining should produce. The attempt to force conformity to such a standard would soon result either in usurpation of the function of management by labor or in an authoritative determination of wage and profits which would be political and arbitrary.[14]

With respect to government price-and-wage surveillance, or price-and-wage fixing, the same point was elaborated on by National Chamber of Commerce economists in testimony before the Senate Subcommittee on Antitrust and Monopoly (Committee on the Judiciary) in these words:

> The free market, in a sense, is a giant automatic calculator which continuously establishes and changes the values of inputs and outputs which in turn, determine how resources are used. Who is presumptuous enough to say he knows the "correct" structure of relative prices at any moment in time? Have our years of experience in tampering with agricultural prices, parities and production engendered in

14. *Annual Proceedings,* Industrial Relations Research Association, December, 1958.

us such confidence that we feel we can now replace the market in other sectors by seeking to impose external, and as yet unspecified criteria?

Furthermore, we would point out that the economic decision-making processes are essentially forward-looking. While past experience in the form of cost and other business records may help, the decision maker must still make his decisions as to output, prices, investment and the like on subjective estimates of the future—growth of markets, impact of prices on sales, probable cost conditions, prospects of entry, etc. Different decision makers will have different time horizons and in different markets various economic forces will operate at different rates of speed to confirm or reject and correct errors in judgment.[15]

Analyses and conclusions like the foregoing can be ignored by a nation only at its peril. While it may be in the interests of union officials to take labor out of the open market, it is not in the public interest. If collective bargaining succeeded in producing that result, it would destroy competition and hence one of the foundation stones on which a free society rests. Fortunately, the open market provides us with a better alternative than arbitrary wage determination by either unions or government. We already rely on the market in the commodity-pricing process.[16] We should rely on it much more in the labor market. The absence of a free labor market was behind the wide endorsement of the controls imposed in 1971.

In searching for some criteria for wage and salary determinations, Dr. Winfield W. Riefler, then assistant to the chairman, Board of Governors of the Federal Reserve System (in an address July 21, 1959, entitled *Inflation—Enemy of Growth*) stated:

... I would hope that the benefits of rising productivity and growth were broadly distributed in three general direc-

15. W. D. Fackler and P. P. Frucht, *Administered Prices and Inflation* (Washington, D.C.: Chamber of Commerce of USA, 1959).

16. William Fellner, *The Problem of Rising Prices* (Paris: Organization for Economic Cooperation and Development, 1961). Concludes that inflation is not caused by administered prices, but by rising wage costs. For further discussion of this report and the problem in general see, E. P. Schmidt's article in *Industrial Relations,* University of California, Berkeley, Cal., May 1962, pp. 43-44.

tions and not overweighted in any one: (a) in the direction of wage and incomes advanced to the working force *to encourage mobility and the ready availability* of needed skills and talents at points of innovation; (b) in the direction of lower prices promotive of broader and expanded markets for those end products where productivity has lowered real costs; and (c) in the direction of sufficient profit-encouragement to those who innovate successfully to stimulate initiative in management-planning for growth. In other words, I would favor a situation where the efficiencies of growth were reflected in falling, not rising, unit costs. . . . (Italics supplied.)

This is quite clearly a plea for making the free market function effectively in the broad general interest and letting market forces distribute the gains of productivity among all groups and sectors of society.[17]

This is, in fact, the process whereby, over the course of history, we have raised our scale of living to the world's highest levels. And it does not entail stagnant real income for workers; it provides rising *real* purchasing power for them—as it should.

But union monopoly, compulsory unionism, and the use of force, violence, and coercion must be eliminated if genuine and balanced collective bargaining, based on discussion and persuasion, is to be restored. The renunciation of the use of force is not unknown. For example, during the many years it was under the leadership of William D. Mahon, the Street-Car Workers' International Union required that all disputes, including contract renewals, be ultimately settled by voluntary arbitration.[18]

---

17. *The New York Times* in an editorial, after the 116-day steel strike of 1959, took this same position: ". . . it should be left to competition and the price system to determine how the income flowing from the process of turning raw materials into finished goods should be distributed . . ." December 5, 1959. For a similar conclusion see the vigorous exposition of Professor Walter D. Fackler of the University of Chicago before a joint session of the American Statistical Association and the American Economic Association, December 30, 1959, *Proceedings* of the former.

18. For this excellent record, see *Industrial Relations in Urban Transportation* by E. P. Schmidt, particularly Chapter 11 (Minneapolis, Minn.: University of Minnesota Press, 1937).

Public sentiment may well force our nation into some form of permanent, coercive government wage and union control, if the key recommendations of this study are ignored. It is easier and better to disperse and diffuse undue concentrations of power (as we have done effectively, if not perfectly, in the product markets through antitrust laws) than it is to try to regulate them.[19]

## STOPPING ANNUAL GENERAL WAGE INCREASES

Without minimizing the key role of proper monetary, credit, and fiscal policies in maintaining sustained noninflationary prosperity, the question may be raised whether any *general* wage increase should be granted by an employer as a result of collective bargaining in a competitive and dynamic economy. The only reason an employer should raise wages is to recruit and hold an adequate supply of workers. If he has difficulty in securing manpower, his pay scale or his management practices may be inadequate; if he has more job applicants than openings, or has no difficulties in hiring, his offering rates are obviously adequate, or more than adequate. Proper wage and salary administration within a specific establishment, however, should also provide for *individual* payment adjustments, based on performance.

Such wage policies in a highly competitive economy, complemented by noninflationary credit and fiscal policies, would help distribute productivity gains over the years and would lead to a stable or a slowly falling general price level. This would benefit all consumers, including workers, those who have retired, and those who are living on fixed and lagging incomes. It would provide an automatic, steady increase in *real* income for the gainfully occupied, as well as for others. And it would help to mitigate our international balance-of-payments problems.

It is difficult to escape the conclusion that, regardless of the conflicting diagnoses and prescriptions and the dissent by union officials, the forces of supply and demand—that is, the free play of

---

19. For more extended analysis of these problems, see *Inflation, Unions and Wage Policy,* Chamber of Commerce of USA, 1960.

open-market forces—should determine wage rates and wage levels. Collective bargaining, devoid—and known to be devoid—of force and compulsion, would be consistent with this goal.

What has been said of wages applies with equal force to prices in the goods market. Competition in the goods market should be enforced, and should be relied upon to pass on the benefits of technical progress and cost reductions to employees and others as consumers. Only if we have effective competition in the goods market, and it is substantially effective, can we expect adequate public support for the foregoing union and wage policies. In protected industries, tariff reductions could be used to augment competitive markets. In public utilities, where monopoly prevails, government regulation may be available. But the recent study, *The Regulated Consumer* by Mary B. Peterson (*op. cit.*), raised serious questions about numerous regulatory agencies, including the NLRB.

And finally, let us repeat the warning of Lord Beveridge:

> If trade unions under full employment press wage claims unreasonably, maintenance of a stable price level will become impossible; wage determination will perforce become a function of the State.

And the warning of John Davenport (*Fortune*, July 1971):

> There must be a final reservoir of coercive power if law and order are to be maintained. That properly belongs to government alone. It must not be farmed out to private parties whether these be unions, corporations, or mobs in the street.

Opposition to the policy changes recommended herein will come from union-centered critics: union officials, all too many labor economists—particularly those who, along with lawyers, are heavily engaged in professional arbitration of labor disputes—and from most politicians who rely on the labor vote. All of these have a vested interest in keeping things as they are. They will do what they can to perpetuate their advantages, but the public should be on guard against any and all self-serving postures, slogans, and words. The public should raise high the principles of equity and justice, and recognize that these are best preserved through the open market, the rule of law, and the decency and orderliness of voluntary, uncoerced decision-making.

This study has not been concerned with all the ills in our society. It is a labor-union study. It has been concerned not only with inflation, but also with the accumulation of uneconomic work practices, and the misallocation of resources that arises because we increasingly lack open labor markets.

Very much has gone wrong with the labor union and with collective bargaining. Nearly all scholars now agree on that point. Our concern has been to focus on these wrongs and suggest corrective policies.

Yet it is clear that without greater fiscal responsibility, more effective limitations on government appropriations and spending, and an effective monetary policy, the struggle to create a humane society with optimal noninflationary economic growth and employment will be in vain.

# APPENDIX

## THERE IS NO MORAL RIGHT TO STRIKE[20]

Rarely challenged is the right to strike. While nearly everyone in the population, including the strikers themselves, will acknowledge the inconvenience and dangers of strikes, few will question the right-to-strike concept. They will, instead, place the blame on the abuses of this assumed right—for instance, on the bungling or ignorance or evil of the men who exercise control of strikes.

The present laws of the United States recognize the right to strike; it is legal to strike. However, as in the case of many other legal actions, it is impossible to find moral sanction for strikes in any creditable ethical or moral code.

This is not to question the moral right of a worker to quit a job or the right of any number of workers to quit in unison. Quitting is not striking, unless force or the threat of force is used to keep others from filling the jobs vacated. The essence of the strike, then, is the resort to coercion to force unwilling exchange or to inhibit willing exchange. No person, nor any combination of persons, have a moral right to force themselves—at their price—on any employer, or to forcibly preclude his hiring others.

Reference need not be confined to moral and ethical codes to support the conclusion that there is no moral right to strike. Anyone's sense of justice will render the same verdict if an employer-employee relationship, devoid of emotional background, is examined.

An individual with an ailment employs a physician to heal him. The physician has a job to do on terms agreeable to both. Our sense of justice suggests that either the patient or the physician is morally warranted in quitting this employer-employee relationship at will, provided that there is no violation of contract. Now, assume that the physician (the employee) goes on strike. His

---

20. Leonard E. Read, *The Coming Aristocracy* (Irvington-on-Hudson, N.Y.: Foundation for Economic Education, 1969). Reproduced with permission.

ultimatum: "You pay me twice the fee I am now getting or I quit! Moreover, I shall use force to prevent any other physician from attending to your ailment. Meet my demands or do without medical care from now on."

Who will claim that the physician is within his moral rights when taking an action such as this? The above, it should be noted, is not a mere analogy but a homology, an accurate matching in structure of the common or garden variety of legalized, popularly approved strike.

To say that one believes in the right to strike is comparable to saying that one endorses monopoly power to exclude business competitors; it is saying, in effect, that government-like control is preferable to voluntary exchange between buyers and sellers, each of whom is free to accept or reject the other's best offer. In other words, to sanction a right to strike is to declare that might makes right—which is to reject the only foundation upon which civilization can stand.

Lying deep at the root of the strike is the persistent notion that an employee has a right to continue an engagement once he has begun it, as if the engagement were his own piece of property. The notion is readily exposed as false when examined in the patient-physician relationship. A job is but an exchange affair, having validity only during the life of the exchange. It ceases to exist the moment either party quits or the contract ends. The right to a job that has been quit is no more valid than the right to a job that has never been held.

The inconvenience to individuals and the dangers to the economy, inherent in strikes, should not be blamed on the bungling or ignorance or evil of the men who manipulate them. Rather, the censure should be directed at the false idea that there is a moral right to strike.

# INDEX